BASKETBALL:
The NBA Coaches Handbook

BASKETBALL:
The NBA Coaches Handbook

Edited by Giorgio Gandolfi

with Gerald Couzens

PRENTICE-HALL, INC.

Englewood Cliffs, N.J.

Prentice-Hall International, Inc., *London*
Prentice-Hall of Australia, Pty. Ltd., *Sydney*
Prentice-Hall Canada, Inc., *Toronto*
Prentice-Hall of India Private Ltd., *New Delhi*
Prentice-Hall of Japan, Inc., *Tokyo*
Prentice-Hall of Southeast Asia Pte. Ltd., *Singapore*
Whitehall Books, Ltd., Wellington, *New Zealand*
Editora Prentice-Hall do Brasil Ltda., *Rio de Janeiro*
Prentice-Hall Hispanoamericana, S.A., *Mexico*

Library of Congress Cataloging-in-Publication Data

Main entry under title:

Basketball, the NBA coaches handbook.

  Bibliography: p.
  1. Basketball—Coaching—Addresses, essays,
lectures.   2. National Basketball Association—
Addresses, essays, lectures.   I. Gandolfi, Giorgio.
II. Couzens, Gerald Secor.   III. Title: NBA coaches
handbook.
GV885.3.B365   1986   796.32′3′077   85-19135

0-13-069469-X

Printed in the United States of America

DEDICATION

To a Special Flight

FOREWORD
By: Red Holzman

The name Red Holzman, is synonymous with NBA tradition and history. Red, an outstanding player under Nat Holman at City College of New York in the early 1940's, broke in to the professional ranks as a player with Rochester of the National League in the 1945-46 season. Since then he has served as player-coach, scout, coach, general manager, and consultant.

After retiring from the coaching reins at the end of the 1981-82 season with the Knickerbockers, Holzman compiled 696 victories, 613 of them with New York. Three times a coach in the NBA championship finals, Red achieved World Championships with the Knickerbockers in 1970 and 1973 and was named Coach of the Year in 1970.

I've had the good fortune to be involved in one role or another in the great game of professional basketball almost since its inception. While the basics of the game have remained essentially the same, the skills of the players and the level of sophistication of the coaching techniques have advanced dramatically.

As the head coach of the World Champion New York Knicks in 1970 and 1973, I had the distinct advantage of observing many of these changes during what many have called the turning point years of the NBA.

Today there are super athletes on every NBA team whose overall ability certainly qualify them as the "greatest athletes in all sports." Very often then it is the coaching of this talent that makes the difference between a winning team and a losing one. Today's NBA coach must be totally well-versed in every aspect of the game, and, just as important, he must have the ability to communicate these concepts to his players and thereafter motivate them to perform. In other words, he must be the ultimate teacher.

Like every great teacher, the NBA coach cannot do the job alone. It is here in this era of great basketball sophistication that the assistant coach has come to play a prominent role alongside the coach.

With the publication of *Basketball: The NBA Coaches Handbook*, head coaches and assistant coaches of the NBA share their knowledge of the game of basketball on a wide range of key topics. This unique opportunity will provide a wealth of information for the basketball coach on every level of the game and for anyone truly interested in learning basketball from the coaches' standpoint.

All of the materials presented have a practical use and the accompanying diagrams explain in detail the information presented. This book, the first in a series, will make an invaluable addition to the sport of basketball and will, I'm sure, be "must" reading for every basketball coach, wherever the game is played.

R.H.

Introduction

Each year in this country many books about basketball play and techniques are written. Most are penned by unknown coaches, while some rare others by famous basketball "gurus." What separates *Basketball: The NBA Coaches Handbook* from all the rest is that for the first time the top coaches in the basketball-playing world, the coaches and assistants of the National Basketball Association, have collected their knowledge into one book. The end result is basketball at its best. *Basketball: The NBA Coaches Handbook* offers an enlightened approach to the game that is packed with information on how a coach can get the best from both the team and individual players. Without a doubt this is the ultimate guide to winning basketball.

Divided into five sections, the book provides useful and simplified coaching strategies that will be of great service to coaches at all levels of the game. Although it's been said that the game of basketball is nothing but a simple children's game made more difficult by a bunch of coaches, *Basketball: The NBA Coaches Handbook* is out to change that impression. The NBA coaches who have contributed to this book have the best players in the world to put their coaching theories into practice. These theories are not effective just because of the NBA players who execute them, but because they are basically sound and simple coaching strategies. And because simplicity is the common denominator, the coaching philosophies found in this book are useful for coaches at all levels of the game.

—Giorgio Gandolfi

ACKNOWLEDGMENTS

This genesis of *Basketball: The NBA Coaches Handbook* begins at the end of December 1976 when I left Italy and landed in New York, for the first time. I was in America to discover what the great game of American basketball was all about and I felt like a space explorer who had just reached Venus. Now the NBA arenas are my second home.

I would like to take this opportunity to thank those who helped me and put me in touch with the fantastic world of this great sport and without whom I couldn't have written this book.

First of all, my parents, Antonio and Tina, Gerald Couzens, New York sports writer, who assisted me in the phases of my work and gave me my first roof in the USA, Chuck Daly, Head Coach of the Detroit Pistons for his friendship and teachings on the game of pro basketball, Bob Zuffelato, Assistant Coach of Golden State Warriors, and Lou Carnesecca, Coach of St. John's University who furthered my teachings.

To the NBA Commissioner, David J. Stern, and his fine staff who have given me the access necessary to explore the world of the NBA.

A special thanks to Michael Goldberg, Executive Director of the National Basketball Coaches Association, for his support and all the great professional NBA coaches who gave me their time and help. And finally, to Roberta Cottica, who with great patience and care drafted the diagrams that are such an integral part of this book.

G.G.

Table of Contents

BASKETBALL:
The NBA Coaches Handbook

Fundamentals
and Principles

THE PRACTICE:
KEY TO AN EFFECTIVE GAME

by Cotton Fitzsimmons

Lowell "Cotton" Fitzsimmons was an All-American guard at
Hannibal-LaGrange College. His first coaching job was at
Moberly Junior College. In 1966 and 1967, his team cap-
tured the national JUCO title and Fitzsimmons was named
coach of the year. Cotton was head coach at Kansas State
for two years, racking up a 34-20 record, a Big Eight title,
and coach-of-the-year honors.

Fitzsimmons moved to the NBA in 1970 as head coach of the
Phoenix Suns. He then spent five seasons with the Atlanta
Hawks, before taking the head coach position at Kansas
City in 1978. He is presently the head coach of the San
Antonio Spurs.

I'm a firm believer that the key to any successful practice
session is organization. It's essential for every coach to know how to
utilize both time and personnel properly. Years ago in the NBA this
wasn't always the case. Since most pro coaches came from the ranks of
former players, they simply followed routines that their coaches had used
with them. But with the influx into the pros over the past 15 years of
successful college coaches who know the value of organization, the
emphasis on organized practices has become the rule, rather than the
exception.

In preparing your practice it's important to know ahead of time the
following three things:

1. What you're going to teach or stress at the workout
2. How you're going to teach and implement your ideas
3. Why you are going to teach and what you want to accomplish from it

Important guides that I've always used in my coaching are "the six honest men of experience": Who, What, When, Where, Why, and How. I consult with them daily when I plan practice. Once I can answer to each of them, I know I have the basis for a good session.

A good guideline in setting up practice should be the amount of time that you have. I like to practice for 90 minutes. Other coaches will go two hours, some even longer. But I'm convinced that if you can keep the players' attention for just 90 minutes, you can gain more positive results than with longer sessions.

Anytime you organize a practice you should try to incorporate as many basic fundamentals into each drill you use as possible. For example, in running a simple lay-up drill, the players should not only make the lay-ups, but also concentrate on good passing, good dribbling, and proper footwork. I always stress these skills.

You can never overemphasize fundamentals! All good coaches will incorporate them into everything they do on the court, no matter what they may be teaching. If a coach allows his players to become careless or sloppy with their passes during lay-ups, he's not only going to foster bad habits (which may cost him some games somewhere down the line), but he's going to have a bad lay-up drill as well. The end result is nothing positive to speak about.

Remember: If you're properly organized, your practices should include the building blocks of good basketball: passing, dribbling, and shooting. Let these be your foundation and you won't go wrong.

Today, I'm coaching exactly the same way I did when I was a junior college coach. When it comes to coaching, the NBA isn't actually too different from college. Sure, the pro players are more talented, bigger, faster, and stronger, but they still need coaching. When I first came to the NBA, I was told that my college-based coaching methods wouldn't work with the pro athlete. "It's never been done that way before," they said. "They're not looking for coaching in the NBA; just get them to the game on time, make sure they have a basketball, and let them play."

This was the furthest thing from the actual situation! I found that the players were not only looking for coaching and direction but they really needed it.

Each and every one of your practice sessions should be a positive and exciting experience and the players should be enthused about coming to work out. As a way of keeping them "up" for practice I rely on *planning* and *variety*. Of course some players have their "off days" and come on the court with a bad attitude. No matter what type of practice I have scheduled, it's not going to change them; for the most part coaches are neither shrinks nor miracle workers and you shouldn't try to be one. In the pro game we play an 82-game schedule that's physically demanding and grueling, so I have to expect some "off" practice days from the players. In the high school or college ranks you can expect off days as well, especially before, during, and after exam periods.

By all means avoid repetition in your practices. If any one thing will kill a practice it's going over the same drills day after day. Under no circumstances should you repeat the same things every day, even if you feel that will help overcome a particular team deficiency. Too much repetition will only lead to dull and boring practices, the end result being that you'll achieve little of what you had initially intended.

I have outlined here a typical pro practice schedule. You should keep in mind that after going through the schedule, I will throw out a few drills and add new ones every two or three days. This is just the right spice needed and seems to keep the players from expecting the same thing every day. I find that if I give the players something new to learn or work on, they'll love it and respond positively.

I start every practice with a stretching regime. Now, I know some of you may want to dismiss this because you think that it doesn't relate directly to basketball. Well, it sure does. Recently the Philadelphia 76ers hired a full-time conditioning coach to lead the team in stretching and warm-up exercises before and after practice. The 76ers (and others as well) believe that this pre-game and post-game conditioning program played a big role in their 1983 NBA Championship title win. Many other pro teams have followed suit and started their own stretching programs.

For years I've been a believer in the benefits of stretching. I find it to be a preventative measure; it will prepare the player for the upcoming practice as well as strengthen his musculoskeletal system and help prevent injuries.

I begin our stretching program with stretching from the top of the head and work down to the toes. Half of the exercises are done in a standing position and the other half while sitting. You stretch basically all the same muscles that you use in the game of basketball.

When we first adopted a prepractice stretch program some of my players resisted primarily because they weren't too flexible, but also because they were embarrassed at not being able to stretch. I have found over the years in coaching that many athletes are afraid to try something new, especially if they may be embarrassed in the trying. A good way around this is to sit your players down and explain to them that a muscle pull, muscle sprain, strain, or tear could knock them out of the lineup or prevent them from working at their full capacity. By stretching, they will greatly reduce the chance of being seriously injured in practice or a game. Although stretching may not prevent a hamstring pull, for example, it will certainly lessen the severity of one. Some of my most reluctant players have become leaders in our stretching program at practice after going injury-free for all or most of the season.

The entire series of prepractice stretching exercises takes only about 17 minutes and is well worth the time spent. There are many books and programs offered by conditioning coaches, and you should seriously investigate them and see which one you want to follow. Once you step up your program, you've taken the first step for a successful practice.

When the stretching is over, you are ready to begin practice.

I normally start off with a passing drill. I teach and review some basic fundamental passes: the two-hand chest pass, two-hand chest bounce pass, two-hand overhead pass (if you use this type of pass for hitting the post), and the two-hand reach-around bounce pass. Although I'm a big believer in the two-hand passes, the baseball pass (an outlet pass thrown one-handed from one end of the floor to the other) is one that shouldn't be ignored. I've seen many games broken open and won when this pass was successfully executed.

Although the baseball pass is an important pass, you'll be surprised and even shocked at the number of pro players who aren't able to make it. When we work at this pass in practice I often close up the gym. With all the poorly thrown passes, I'm afraid that some spectators may be injured by a loose ball.

One important thing to remember about the passing drills: Keep them exciting and change them every two or three days.

At the end of the passing drills and without stopping the practice, we move right into the lay-up drill. My lay-up drill is a little different from others around. I call it a "ten angles" drill and use it at every practice. It's called "ten" or "ten angles" simply because the players shoot lay-ups in different ways and from different angles on the floor. All of these lay-ups are actual types of shots that the players will use during the course of a game.

The shooting drill is the third drill of the practice. I want to emphasize that I don't like my players to come out before practice and start to shoot around with the ball. The reasons for this are simple:

1) They haven't had a chance to stretch and properly warm up.
2) Shooting casually, lofting up soft shots, certainly doesn't represent any game-type situation and is really a waste of time.
3) If allowed to continue it could easily lead to developing poor game habits.

For my first shooting drill, two players work together. One of them rebounds, passes the ball, and closes the other out. Working under these conditions is similar to game conditions, and the players get the benefit from shooting at different angles on the court.

A good way to work the drill is to have both the forwards and centers shooting not only with their backs to the basket, but also facing the backboard. Again, this is not only something different, but more closely similar to game conditions.

The shooting guards should work on different shots. The quick jump shot from the 15- to 18-foot range is often practiced. I also have them fake a shot, take a few dribbles, and take a jumper from a shorter range. Or they may fake a shot and drive straight to the basket. I like to have the guards and small forwards shoot different shots from various angles, but always from places on the court they will normally shoot from during the game.

This shooting drill takes eight minutes. I don't believe in long drills, but in ones that take three to ten minutes at the maximum. *Remember:* Longer drills only result in boredom and loss of excitement. So practice a drill, reach the high pitch of excitement and enthusiasm, then quickly change the drill and move right on to something else.

Following the shooting drill, I usually have a list of things that I need to cover that day. For example, if our next game is against a real fast break team, I will run drills for stopping that element of their game. This is done by clamping down on the rebounder; playing the outlet pass; crashing the boards, sometimes with four players moving in for the offensive rebound; and sending the first two men to the defensive basket.

Rebounding is critical in every game, so I generally work on this at each practice. I will pair up the players two on two, throw the ball up to the glass, and like gladiators of old, they have to fight to get the ball. Then I go three on three, four on four, and five on five. If the offensive team just touches the ball, they get a point. If they tip the ball, they receive 3 points. If they rebound and make the basket, they get 4 points. If the defensive team rebounds the ball, they start the fast break to the other end of the court and the team which was on offense must make the quick transition. This is just one way I have turned a fundamental drill into a game situation which is both competitive and exciting for the players.

My coaching philosophy is that when we run an offensive play every player should know exactly what each player on the team has to do. Therefore, I like to break every play down step by step and run it over many times without defense so everyone can see what's going on. From this type of drill I'm not only working on my offense, but on overall conditioning as well.

I always end my practices with something positive. If there is one thing that players love to do, it's scrimmage, so that's how I generally finish up.

I'm always looking for a competitive scrimmage. In order to insure it, I have it run for either a quarter or 30 points, whichever comes first. Sometimes we play with the losers having to buy a meal for the winners or else they pay for dessert. This makes the scrimmage even more competitive because one thing the players hate to give up is money.

Whenever I notice that the players are struggling, fouling too much, and throwing away too many balls, I look for the right moment to end the practice. Timing here is important and should focus on something positive or exciting: a great offensive move, a dunk, or a steal. Even if the time limit or scoring total hasn't been reached, I'll end the practice. The players can now leave the gym excited and in an "up" mood. Proper attitude is the key to all performance.

Before heading for the showers the players cool down with 12 minutes of post-practice stretching.

SAMPLE PRACTICE SESSION

Morning

11–11:17 a.m.—Stretching exercises (the coach leads the players)

11:17–11:26 a.m.—The passing drills.

Four Corners Drill: Diagram 1-1. The players line up in four lines in the corners of the half court. 01 passes the ball to 04 and follows the pass. 04 gives the ball back to 01. The same movement happens on the other line with a pass from 07 to 010.

8

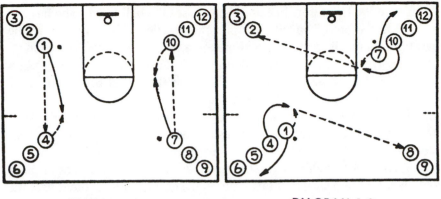

DIAGRAM 1-1   DIAGRAM 1-2

Four Corners Drill: Diagram 1-2. 01 makes a one-count stop and pivots for a handoff pass to 04. After passing the ball, 01 goes to the end of the line. 07 and 010 will make the same movement. In this drill, you can use different types of passes and also work on footwork.

11:26 a.m.–11:34 a.m.—Lay-Up Drill–All Angles

Lay-Up All Angles Drill: Diagram 1-3. The players line up in two lines on the two sides of the half court. 01 dribbles in to shoot a lay-up shot. 04 takes the rebound, dribbles parallel to the baseline, and passes to 02, who cuts to the basket and makes a righthand straight lay-up. **Note:** It's important to the success of this drill that the rebounder make a proper pass, either a lateral bounce pass or a two-hand chest pass.

Lay-Up All Angles Drill: Diagram 1-4. There are two lines of players: one under the basket and the other near the out-of-bounds line. 01

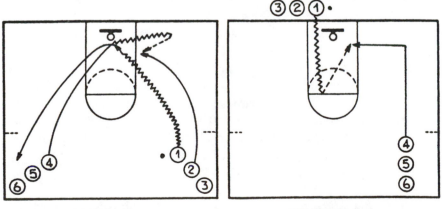

DIAGRAM 1-3   DIAGRAM 1-4

dribbles to the free throw line and then passes the ball to 04, who has run parallel to the out-of-bounds line and then made a 90-degree cut to the baseline. 04 receives the ball and makes a lay-up using the left hand.

Lay-Up All Angles Drill: Diagram 1-5. There are two lines of players: one under the basket and the other near the out-of-bounds line. 01 dribbles to the free throw line and then passes the ball to 04, who has made the same type of cut seen before. 04 makes one dribble and shoots under the basket on the other side, using the rim as help against the shot blocker. He makes a movement up and then under the basket.

Lay-Up All Angles Drill: Diagram 1-6. There are two lines of players: one near the basket (but this time on the court), and the other near the out-of-bounds line. 01 dribbles parallel to the baseline and when he is out of the lane, he passes the ball to 04, who after faking to make a cut on the sideline, crosses over at the free throw line and explodes to the basket.

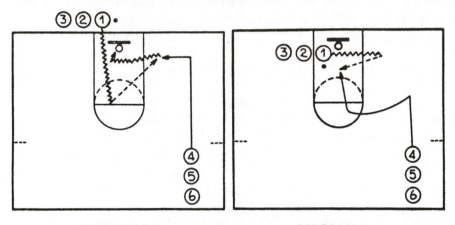

DIAGRAM 1-5   DIAGRAM 1-6

Lay-Up All Angles Drill: Diagram 1-7. There are two lines of players, set up the same way as before. 01 dribbles parallel to the baseline and when he is out of the lane, he passes the ball to 04, who, after faking to make a cut on the sideline, crosses over. In this case, 04 makes one dribble so he can use the backboard and the rim against the defender. The same five lay-ups are made on the left side of the half court. With this simple drill, the players can work on all types of lay-ups that they can expect to execute during the course of a game.

11:34 a.m.–11:42 a.m.—Individual Shooting Drill

Individual Shooting Drill: Diagram 1-8. The players are paired. 01 are the point guards who work not only on driving to the basket, but also on jump shots. 02 are the shooting guards, who not only work on the

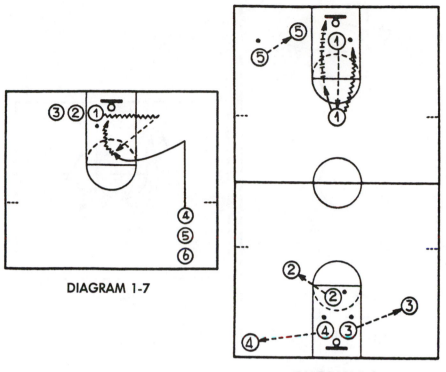

DIAGRAM 1-7

DIAGRAM 1-8

jump shot from a range of 15–18 feet, but also on a range of the 3-point shot as well. 03 are the small forwards, who make the jump shot from the corners and work on the 3-point shot. 04 are the power forwards, who shoot with their backs to the basket and also facing the basket. 05 work inside, because these are the big men. They can also come out for the jump shot. One player passes the ball and then follows to contest the shot. The shooter goes to the rebound and makes the same move.

11:42–11:52 a.m.—Outlet Pass and Fast Break Drill

11:52 a.m.–12:10 p.m.—Fast break drills

1. Two lines
2. Three lines
3. Four lines
4. Five lines

Fast Break After a Successful Free Throw Drill: Diagram 1-9. We use this drill for teaching the player how to score after a successful free throw made by the opponent. 02, the scoring guard, and 03, the small

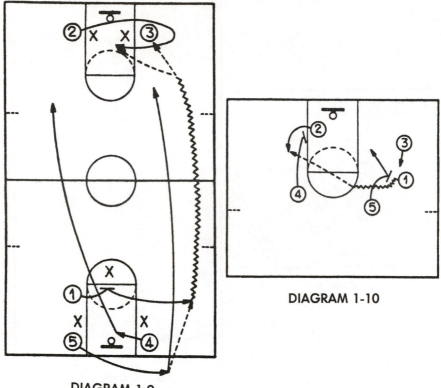

DIAGRAM 1-10

DIAGRAM 1-9

forward, line up at the low post position at the offensive end of the court. 05 makes the out-of-bounds pass to 01, who after blocking out the free throw shooter, goes to receive the ball near the sidelines. 04 must go for the defensive rebound. It is his responsibility to free up 01 so he can receive the ball, or receive the ball himself if 01 is covered. He then releases and goes on the left lane.

01 dribbles as fast as possible to the free-throw line extended and attempts to give the ball to 02, who uses the screen of 03; or 01 may also pass to 03.

Fast Break After a Successful Free Throw Drill: Diagram 1-10. If there isn't any solution, 04 comes down and screens for 02, who curled and comes out of the three seconds area, while 05 screens for 01 and then rolls to the basket. 01 has different options: he can pass the ball to 02, to 05, or 04, who cuts in the lane after the pick.

12:10–12:35 p.m.—Free throw shooting

It's important that the players all concentrate when they take free throws. I like to appoint someone to keep track of the daily percentages.

12:20–12:35 p.m.—Scrimmage

The team is divided into two units, the blue and white, each with two forwards, two guards, one center.

PLAYBACK

1) Organization is the key to a successful practice.
2) Know ahead of time what you plan to teach, how you plan to implement your ideas, and what you hope to accomplish from each practice.
3) 90-minute practice sessions that incorporate all the fundamentals into every drill are sufficient. Some coaches may like to go longer but they risk boring the players.
4) Variety is the key to an interesting practice. Under no circumstance should you repeat the same drills day after day.
5) Use a stretching program before and after practice. It will pay off with fewer and less severe injuries during the season.
6) Make every drill in practice duplicate a game situation. Don't let players shoot lazily at the basket before practice; it's not a game situation and will only foster bad habits.
7) End all practices on something positive, even cutting practice short to achieve this.

TEACHING INDIVIDUAL FUNDAMENTALS OF FOOTWORK AND BALANCE

by Pete Newell

In 21 years of college coaching at the University of San Francisco, Michigan State, and U. Cal, Berkeley, Pete Newell compiled an amazing .657 winning percentage, guiding teams to both NCAA and NIT championships. In 1960 he guided the U.S. Olympic basketball team to a gold medal performance in Rome. In that same year, Cal went 28-1 and Newell was named College Coach of the Year.

Newell was General Manager of the Los Angeles Lakers from 1972–76 and currently is a talent consultant for the Golden State Warriors.

The game of basketball is conditioned by rules and their interpretations. Because of the necessity for a delicate balance between the value of the ball and the penalty of the foul, basketball rules are in constant adjustment. If the rules themselves don't change often their interpretations do. It's the wise coach who is conscious of every change of rule or interpretation and prepares his team accordingly.

The college and high school game has important differences from the NBA. Two rules, principally, create the main variances between the two games. These two rules are the 24-second clock and the no-zone rule. These NBA rules shape their game much differently than the college-high school game. Because of their differences, there is a chasm that must be bridged by all college players coming into the NBA and it's very difficult for many. Some bridge it early, some late, some never.

Two college rules and interpretations caused drastic changes in the coaching of the college game in the 1960's, rules that slowly but inevitably changed the styles of offense and defense the coaches employed. These changes were the *charge interpretation* and the *screen interpretation*. The charge interpretation caused offenses to depend more on a perimeter shot and not risk the offensive charge foul. Defensive players were taught how to cleverly cause the charge of the offensive man. College offenses changed from systems that created shots flashing to the basket with or without the ball, to a perimeter shot created away from the ball with the help of the down or side screen. This type of offense became known as the *motion* or *passing* game. The liberalization of the offensive screen rule and the close calling of the offensive charge caused this rebirth of the motion offense. Coach Hank Iba, a number of years ago, made this type of offense popular but it too had become a victim of rule changes and interpretations.

The screen interpretation change related to rights of a screener and the defensive man. The screener wasn't permitted to be in movement inside 3 feet of the defensive man he was screening. Any contact was presumed to be the fault of the screener. The defensive man was permitted, theoretically, one step, which would allow him to move around the screen.

In the mid-60's the screener was given more rights, the defensive man less. The screener could move within inches of the defensive man and more contact was permitted. Often contact was never called. Today the great majority of teams use some type of motion offense. I've noticed a trend toward protecting the driver from the charge and the defensive man from the moving screen. If the trend continues, offensive concepts will again slowly but inevitably change.

Another byproduct of this liberalization of the screen interpretation is the wide use of the zone defense at the high school and college level. Motion type offenses became very difficult to defend without getting into foul trouble. The coaches met this problem by going to multiple defenses. The multiple defense is a combination of a man-to-man defense and a zone defense or a number of different zone defenses. The zone defense will usually neutralize a strong screening offense. What I've described is a college game that creates a shot away from the ball and defense that's basically zone in nature. The college game is a much different type game than is played in the NBA.

The purpose of giving this background of the college game is to emphasize the difference between the college and pro game. Defensively, the games differ a great deal. The zone defense that many colleges employ differs fundamentally from the man defense the NBA plays. The zone is played in a more straight-legged position, vision is on the ball, responsibility is in an area of the court, the mental qualifications are more passive in nature and responsibility is less defined in defensive rebounding. Further, the responsibility of beating a cutter, anticipating offensive movement, and communication differ from the man-to-man defensive responsibilities. There isn't the same emphasis on foot movement and low stance.

The man-to-man defense demands peripheral or midpoint vision, a low stance that should anticipate offensive cutting to the ball, and mental qualifications that call for initiative, aggressiveness, alertness, and resourcefulness. Pinpoint responsibility by assigning the player to a definite man and definite rebounding responsibility, with great emphasis on foot movement and low stance.

Defensively the adjustment from college ball to the NBA is probably greater than offensively. The player must be able to move with a strong driver and maintain position, fight a back, or sidescreen on or off the ball and general play that is more physical than a new player probably ever encountered previously. Also, checking a rebounder who must be screened and defending a player in a one-on-one situation who is close to unguardable, are just two of several other problems the NBA rookie encounters as he adjusts from college basketball to the NBA.

Additional transition problems occur for the rookie in the NBA as he adjusts from offense to defense. It's much different than a retreat to a zone defense and much more difficult. The college players who come from straight-man defensive teams have much less adjustment to the NBA defensive scheme but not many colleges play straight man defense.

The college player coming into the NBA has many offensive adjustments to make as well. Again there are variances in each game that dictate style differences. In the NBA it's important for the player to learn to screen on the ball, be able to use a screen if they have the ball, create a decent shot in a one-on-one situation, not overdribble the ball and stagnate the offense, and be able to constantly move with or without the ball. The NBA game is structured by the 24-second clock and the "no-zone" concept. The college game is conditioned by its rules that permit the zone defense, some use of the clock (but not a 24-second clock), a closer officiated game, and a much more tactical and strategic type game. College is more of a coach's game, the NBA more of a player's game.

I've prefaced my summer clinic drills with these explanations of the college game and the NBA game to better explain why I teach what I teach.

17

Basketball is a game of foot movement. It's also a game of balance. While a basketball player may only have his hands on the ball 10% of the time, very few basketball players realize this and spend little or no time refining their foot movements and skills. We constantly here references to players "out of control" and yet little time is spent on improving balance. The ability to quickly stop under control, to change direction while under fast speed, change pace or accelerate speed, pivot with either foot as the pivot foot, and jump under good control, are but some of the necessary foot movements that all NBA players are expected to perform. It's my experience that too few drills are aimed at refining their footwork. This is one of the principal reasons for my workouts.

Few players are naturally ambidextrous. Most players are dominantly righthanded or lefthanded, rightfooted or leftfooted. Some players are so comfortable moving in a right direction, they rarely move left. Some are natural going left and seldom go right. I'm referring to their footwork and balance. If they're predominantly rightfooted, they want to take off on that foot and go right. Going left they're not comfortable stopping on their left foot and they shoot less accurately. The reason, usually, is because they don't plant their feet as well and as a result float laterally on their shot. Their balance suffers. Our summer drills attempt to eradicate or reduce this problem by having the drills repeated each day on opposite sides of the court. This will cause a change of pivot from right to left or vice versa each day. It will also require different step-off feet and different directional moves and stops each day. As familiarity and confidence is gained by the player on his weaker foot, his balance will improve. His capacity for moving with greater control, stopping with better balance, and ability to drive in different directions increase his effectiveness as a player. Obviously, if he can move laterally better on offense his defense will improve. Defense starts with position and position implies foot position and movement.

Balance is a word that has more connotations in basketball than any single word I know: Floor balance, team shooting balance, rebound balance, body balance, shooting balance between offense and defense, and balance of personnel. I don't know of any balance more important than that attributed to and necessary for proper footwork.

Unfortunately, in basketball we can't create good footwork and balance with a piece of chalk. It can't be accomplished by pleadings, threats, or demands by the coach. Films won't cause change, and you can't shame a player into proper footwork. Early in my coaching career I found none of the above methods would improve foot skills. I concluded that a physical response can only be cultivated by a repetitive physical act.

18

Because the game of basketball should be played in a low stance, I devised drills that caused the player to move in various directions in a low, fixed knee stance. I increase the time duration of the drills so that players are compelled to stay in this low position in spite of being physically drained. It's important that the basketball player keep his physical composure in spite of fatigue. Games are won and lost in the later stages when fatigue becomes a factor. By learning to stay in a low position, players will be more dependable in critical parts of the game.

Footwork and balance relate to every part of a basketball player's game. The most important single skill in basketball is facility in shooting. The game is decided by the amount of times the ball goes through the hoop. When shooting is explained at clinics, much emphasis is placed on hand position, squaring of the shoulders, follow-through, and shot selection. All of these fundamentals are important. Yet without a good base and proper balance, the shooter would be ineffective in spite of the fundamentals described.

Good balance will insure the lift of the jump shooter to be straight upward. Without a good base and balance, the shooter will often sway or float. To use naval gunnery terms, let me further explain. Deviation and declination are the terms applied in gunnery. Deviation is the lateral adjustment, declination is the depth adjustment. If you have just one adjustment, depth, you have an advantage over the shooter who has a lateral as well as a depth adjustment. To rid a shooter of the deviation or lateral adjustment, the development of footwork and improved balance will reduce or eliminate the lateral float.

Body balance and footwork are necessary requisites in creating a lead to receive a pass. Indirection of movement is dependent upon good foot movement. Regardless of the ability of a player to shoot, he must first receive the ball. At our camp we work hard to develop various foot movements to deploy the defensive man in such a manner that he allows the pass. Spacing or operational zones are extremely important facets of any coach's offense, so it's absolutely necessary for the offensive player to receive the ball within these zones of spacing. The defense is taught to deny this pass within this spacing; therefore, the need for good faking and movement by the offensive man is critical.

Body control is particularly necessary in a foot movement game. "Out of control" is a term used to describe the player prone to mistakes in movement; i.e., offensive charges, progress calls, fumbled balls, and the inability to properly execute a stop. Without proper weight carriage and balance of footwork, good body control is difficult to achieve. Only constant drills and time can improve body control.

The slower type game also demands good body control, so either game tempo—fast or slow—demands attention to this fundamental of movement.

I'll describe some of the drills I teach in my summer practices for NBA players. My purpose is to refine skills, not teach them. The players participate voluntarily to better learn and understand the game of basketball. I find their receptiveness and response very gratifying. I appreciate their professionalism toward their careers.

In teaching basketball, I feel it's extremely important to give attention to every detail. A simple fake must be stressed in order to create the habit of a fake response. I believe in the overfake in order to more deeply implant the habit. A low body base is important in every phase of basketball play and it must be echoed by the teacher or coach. If the coach is permissive in allowing lapses in this basic fundamental of movement, he'll be victimized in the later stages of a game by the lock-kneed, straight-up player.

The demand for the fundamental arm position is another area that requires repetitive vocal reminders by the coach. A player needs to maintain an arm position of up and away from the body for several reasons. Ball reception, fending off a close screener, keeping touch contact with the offensive man by the defensive man, altering the course of a cutter, being arm positioned for rebounds on either board (and not having arms pinned in a crowd around the hoop), are just some of the reasons. Additionally, a player will play with better balance if he has his arms up and away from his body.

I've discussed the simplest of fundamentals above, but their importance can't be questioned. One of the most important tenets of coaching is paying attention to detail. In my summer NBA drills, I stress these details: The proper reception of the ball, the correct foot and body position upon reception, the protection of the ball, the proper turns by the receiver as he faces up, the position of the ball in the face-up, and the vision of the receiver as he looks at the basket. These are simple but important basics of offensive basketball. In each drill I use, I will explain the "why" of the drill. Each fundamental I stress will also be explained.

BALL RECEPTION DRILL

My initial drill is a ball reception drill. The receiver is positioned in an area about 5 feet from the baseline midway between the basket and the sideline.

There are numerous reasons for this position. I call it the *forward's initial position in half court offense*. From this position the receiver can flash to the foul line (for blind pig type action), cut low to the opposite side (should the ball enter from guard to forward on the opposite side), or create a good lead (should the guard on his side beat his man on a drive, he can easily vacate and give his guard an open side).

The passer in this drill is stationed in the normal strongside guard operational zone of a two-guard front. A coach can be the passer because I don't use a defense in this drill.

Timing is a word we often hear and often use in basketball. How do you accomplish this important offensive facet between the passer and cutter? In this drill I strongly stress its importance and again the "why." A cutter can be open but the passer can't deliver the ball because he's dribbling or not positioned to deliver it. The passer in this drill dribbles the ball in a stationary position. The receiver must move along the baseline, faking but not coming out to his forward operational zone. When the receiver sees the passer's second hand go to the ball, he fakes and quickly comes to his receiving position. The passer has now picked up the ball and can deliver it with proper timing. The backdoor mover becomes more of a threat also because of this timing.

To complete this drill the receiver is required to use his inside foot as the pivot foot. The inside foot is that closest to the center of the court as he receives the ball from the passer. *I don't allow any deviation from this inside foot as the pivot foot.*

Again, the why. With the inside foot as the pivot, the receiver can:

a. Better protect the ball as he half-turns to face up to the basket.

b. Execute a deep reverse-step to the basket, should he be faced with an aggressive, denial type defensive man, and drive baseline to the basket. He can drive his defensive man off him with this drive threat and come back to face-up position off this reverse-step.

c. Hand the ball off with a nice low base, and at the same time provide a screen for a circling teammate for a handoff reception.

d. After the face-up, end up at least 4 feet closer to the hoop as he faces up. These 4 feet might be the difference between a 50% range shot or a 30% range shot.

e. Make the defensive man better respect the outside shot potential. This simply means a tighter play which helps create a better pass situation and a drive situation.

The outside foot as the pivot can:

a. Cause steals by the defense because ball protection isn't as good.

b. Offers no reverse threat against a tough play.

c. Provides a terrible handoff position for a teammate.

d. Allows a loss of 4 feet as the receiver squares up to the hoop.

e. Because of this 4-foot loss of distance the defensive man is looser, creating passing and driving problems for the offense.

In this drill, the receiver must face up to the hoop with the ball in a chest-high position and eyes to the basket. The ball in a chest-high position allows for a quick shot, a quick pass, or a drive to the basket. If the ball is carried too low, the defense will respect only the drive and back off. The drive then often becomes a charge. If he immediately goes over his head with the ball, the defensive man will close in because he doesn't respect the drive. This tight play often causes forced passes or balls knocked loose from the offensive man.

With the ball at chest level, the receiver offers the threat of the shot, pass, or drive; therefore, normal play by the defensive man.

The fundamental of passer vision today in college ball varies a great deal from passer vision of decades past. The motion type offense demands the passer read the screener and cutter as soon as the passer receives the ball. Most college teams play some type of motion so this is the vision fundamental usually taught at that level. The NBA demand of vision conforms to the same demands last taught about 15 years ago. The passer or receiver looks at the basket and he can create the three threats of pass, shoot, or drive.

With the 24-second clock of the NBA, it's incumbent upon the offensive man to always present the same threat of the three. Yesterday the drive was more a part of the college game, so it was an inviolate fundamental—"look at the hoop."

In most instances, the younger players I teach have to correct their vision problem because they're generally a day late and a dollar short in being able to create a decent shot. If a player quickly looks to the hoop as he faces up, he creates an almost involuntary defensive reaction to close in on the ball. This allows an easier drive penetration for the offensive man. Conversely, if he looks at the weak side initially, the defensive man will adjust more cautiously.

Simple as these basics seem, they're all a necessary part of an effective NBA player.

ONE-ON-ONE DRILL

I now add a defensive man to the receiver. This defensive man is asked to play tough, denial defense. Good habits of defense will be created by playing this way in practice.

The basic fundamentals of individual man defense in playing the ball are *position, stance*, and *vision*. These are the physical requirements of playing the ball. There are mental requirements of *determination, initiative, resourcefulness, anticipation*, and *aggressiveness* that are equally important. Both the mental and physical requirements are stressed in each drill. If the habits are not created at the practice level, they won't be developed. They're not acquired at a friendly fireside chat, but only with aggressive, repetitive acts.

The most important physical requirement in my view is position. Simply defined, position is the player's relationship between the ball and the basket. When playing the ball of an offensive driver, the movement of feet is of extreme importance. It's more natural, probably much easier actually, to reach with the outside hand to defend a drive. But when a defensive player reaches with the outside hand, he immediately loses foot movement and balance. He then risks a hooking foul or a missed snap at the ball. This usually results in an unopposed drive to the hoop.

Whichever course the defensive player takes is a result of his practice habits. Again, it's a physical reaction that's been conditioned by repetitive acts. If the coach constantly allows the reach, it will become a habit. The coach can rant and rave all he wants, but it won't change the habit.

I *demand* that the inside foot facing the offensive man be in a forward position; a staggered stance with the outside foot back be adopted; the inside hand is up, the opposite hand and arm away from the body.

The purpose of this foot-and-hand position is to defend the vulnerable side better, protect the baseline (where there usually isn't any help), and present the weaker side to the middle (where there usually is help). It's generally accepted in basketball teaching that the more vulnerable side of a defensive man is the side where his foot is extended. Further, if the offensive man commences the drive in either direction, the inside hand is used to snap at the ball but not overcommit. Actually the forearm of this snapping inside hand can impede the path of the driver without much risk of a defensive foul. Both the snap and the use of forearm don't impede the balance or the foot movement of the defensive man.

As I've said before, *balance and foot movement are sacrificed if the outside hand is used to snap at the ball.*

Vision at the chest of the offensive man with the ball is also imperative. Don't be mesmerized by the movement of the ball, the foot faking, or the eyes of the driver. The trunk of the body is more or less steady regardless of other movement, so the eyes should be focused in that area.

HANDS-UP DRILL

Early in my coaching career, I found a number of constant fundamental precepts that never change. Many years later, I'm more certain than ever before about them. I used to talk about stance and movement of feet and their importance, but I came to the realization that either I wasn't a very persuasive talker or it had to be done another way. I deduced it was a physical reaction I wanted, so I needed a physical drill to bring this about. I don't claim authorship of the "hands-up" drill, but I sure made it popular in the west several decades back. It's still used in many parts of the country.

The hands-up drill is a simple shuffle drill. Because the players hate it, it made me better realize its worth. It's a conditioning drill primarily, but it creates the proper court movement for both offense and defense. For the players it's dull, painful, demanding, and boring because of its repetition. It will give the coach a real vocal workout as well.

At the college level, I've worked up to a 20-minute, no-stop drill. High school limits should not exceed 12-14 minutes. In a 10-day period, I have my NBA players progress up to 10 minutes. Once the competitive season begins, I would discontinue the drill's use because it might lead to slow reaction time and tighten the muscles. When employed in the early stages of conditioning, the drill will create the important habit of stance and movement.

Proper stance means a low base, knees flexed, with proper distance and balance of the feet. This drill demands this stance and will cause the habit of the stance to be formed. More importantly, it will strengthen the calf and upper leg muscles. The arms and their support are also strengthened because they're required to be kept up in a regular defensive guarding position.

There's a boxing axiom which states that when the arms are lowered the head takes punishment. In basketball when the hands are lowered the team takes punishment. Without exercising these arm support muscles it's difficult to keep the arms up over a minute without a natural desire to drop them down.

The hands-up drill is conducted over the entire surface of the court. Spacing of the players is in rows, the rows 10 feet apart and each player 10 feet from each side of each other. I use vocal calls for direction change. The direction calls are forward, rear, left, or right. I vary the cadence and the direction constantly. I want the players to react as a group and not try to determine direction.

We start with a regular defensive stance, left foot forward, left hand up, right foot back, and right hand away from the body parallel to the floor. Each day I change the forward foot and hand. When we reach the eight-minute level, I'll change the forward foot and hand. I don't allow a stop.

Also, each day I add a minute to the drill until I reach the goal I set: 20 minutes college; 12-14 high school; and 10 minutes NBA. In college I'd run the drill over a three-week period. Amount of preseason practice time rookie players had in high school would determine how long I ran the drill. My NBA players go for 10 minutes only because I have 10 days with them. When performing the drill, it's important to exhort the players for a fixed knee and raised arm. The knees will stiffen and the arms will drop as the players tire. But conditioning is never easy if it's to be meaningful, so get them to keep their arms up!

Some of the many benefits derived from this drill are:

a. Creates habit of movement.
b. Builds strength and stamina to maintain stance.
c. Causes the player to learn how to reach down and not give in to physical exhaustion.
d. Allows the player to get a better image of himself because he really wants to quit the drill but instead "guts it out."
e. Creates great squad feeling. Teammates know that they've endured the drill equally.

One last reminder on man defense. I use a one-on-one drill that will not allow the use of hands by the defensive man. He must depend solely on the movement of his feet. Again, I'm trying to develop the proper sequence of defensive play: *feet first, hands last*.

In the pro and college game, many coaches and players believe the emphasis on ability to jump has reduced the need for screening. This is faulty reasoning. To emphasize the need and habit of screening, I have the defensive man screen after the shot. He's asked to forget the ball and to set and maintain the proper screen stance. What this hopefully will create is the *screen first, ball second* habit. Only through repetitive acts will this habit be developed.

Offensively, we attempt to do many things in this one-on-one drill. I have added the denying, aggressive defensive man to make the drill more effective.

Many times good perimeter shooters and drivers are forced out of their normal effective range by aggressive defense. When this happens the defense invites the shot and encourages a charge foul.

What we work for in the drill is for the receiver to catch the ball in his normal effective range in spite of a denial defense that's trying to prevent this. We use four basic movements to combat denial:

1) The receiver, in the normal starting position in the vicinity of the baseline puts his inside leg across the legs of the defensive man, pins him momentarily and angles for the pass in his operational zone.

2) If the defense is playing on top with little or no ball vision, he circles him and comes to the receiving area. By circling, I mean going underneath to the foul lane area and proceeding over the top of him to the receiving position.

3) Come to the receiving zone and quickly kick off the outside foot for a back door.

4) Using the same maneuver as 3), except when the defensive man quickly retreats to stop the back door, the receiver pivots and positions himself with the defensive man behind him. He then proceeds to the operational zone.

The greater a player is the more he must learn to combat denial. By the use of these four moves, he has a counter for any type of individual denial he may receive. It's important for a player to learn how to beat tough, aggressive defense in practice so that in a game he'll not be confused by it.

To repeat, the better the defensive contests in practice, the more he helps his offensive teammate improve.

We supplement this basic one-on-one drill with individual skill movements of offense. We practice them without a defense initially and then apply them against a defense.

a) *Reverse-turn and drive to the basket:* This is a basic basketball skill but not many players in the game today can execute the move. It's important that the driver steps toward the basket as he makes his reverse turn. It could be described as a 180-degree turn. If he steps toward the baseline but not toward the basket, he takes a circuitous route. The ball should not be dropped for the drive until the pivot is completed. Many times the ball is dropped too soon and the speed of the move is lessened. Against a tough defensive man, a threat of a reverse will drive him off the ball and allow the offensive man to fake the reverse and face up. He can only loosen this defense with a real threat of a reverse-drive, not just the pivot itself. Some NBA players are now starting all their offensive movement with the reverse-pivot and are comfortable doing it this way.

b) *Rocker step move:* This is a good offensive weapon that's not easy to execute properly. Once it is mastered, though, it gives the offensive man a real advantage. It's simply a step-off move with the upper torso indicating a move back to the original position, and then a quick drive to the basket. What's of utmost importance in teaching this move is the weight position of the feet. As the offensive player makes his step-off, he keeps his weight equally balanced. When his upper torso moves back, his lower weight and balance don't change. His upper-torso fake back is to get a weight commitment forward by the defensive man. The defensive man's weight and direction is going away from the basket. This step isn't easy to master, but a real weapon for the offensive player.

c) *Step-Off fake:* I believe that forwards in basketball need changes of speed to complement their game. The step-off fake is one of these speed changes. It's simply executed by a slow step-off. As soon as the step-off foot hits the floor, the back foot explodes with a drive to the hoop. It initially looks like a slow move, but actually it's a rapid, speed move. With proper timing and situation, it's especially effective against a soft or lazy defensive player. Also, players who use arms instead of feet on defense are vulnerable.

I constantly refer to habits, good and bad. One habit I often face and try to eliminate is the presumption of the offensive man. Some players predetermine what they are going to do before they get the ball. It's a dangerous habit. The defense should always dictate the offensive reaction. I've devised a drill to change this bad reaction.

READING DRILL

Start with the normal one-on-one denial drill. However, the coach will indicate by signal how the defense will play. It will be a) tight denial; b) soft and loose; c) overplay baseline; d) overplay to the middle.

When the receiver gets the ball, he must react in the following manner. If it's a), he reverse-drives to the hoop; b) he immediately shoots; c) he drives to the middle; or d) he drives baseline.

This drill causes a player to change his priorities completely if he's a presumer. He must read and react. The player will learn how to better counter a certain defense. It quickens his reflexes and reactions to these game-type situations. Just because a player is an accomplished NBA player doesn't mean he's above practicing the basics and attempting to learn more and better ways to do things.

PLAYBACK

1) Today's game is overcoached and undertaught. Basketball is a game of balance and foot movement, yet little time is spent on improving these skills. By simple repetitive fundamental drills we keep the game simple and learn proper execution.

2) If the coach is permissive in allowing lapses in teaching basic fundamentals of movement, he'll be victimized in later stages of a game by lock-kneed, straight-up players.

3) Players need to maintain an arm position of up and away from the body. Ball reception, fending off a close screener, keeping touch contact with the offensive man by the defensive man, altering the course of the cutter, being arm positioned for rebounds on either board are just some of the reasons.

4) The basic fundamentals of individual man defense in playing the ball are position, stance, and vision. These habits are created in practice.

5) Screening after a shot is of utmost importance. Defensive players should forget the ball after a shot and screen the offensive player, then go in for the rebound. Only through repetitive acts in practice will this habit be developed.

6) The better the defense contests in practice, the more he helps his offensive teammates improve.

OFFENSIVE PRINCIPLES

by Chuck Daly

Chuck Daly has achieved coaching success in basketball from high school level up through the pro ranks. In his six seasons as head coach of the University of Pennsylvania (1971–77), his Quakers won four Ivy League titles and three Big Five championships.

Daly was the Philadelphia 76ers assistant coach from 1977–81, head coach of the Cleveland Cavaliers in the 1981–82 season, and is currently the head coach of the Detroit Pistons. In 1984 and 1985, Daly guided the Pistons to a playoff berth and his team is now regarded as one of the NBA's most exciting and talented clubs.

The improvement of players year after year, both physically and technically, along with the use of more sophisticated defenses, has brought about many changes in the way pro basketball is played. I would like to touch briefly on some of the significant offensive principles now used in the NBA.

SECONDARY BREAKS

Over the years the running game has changed drastically in the pros. Everyone is aware of the well-defined principles of the two-on-one or the three-on-two fast break. However, I and other coaches look for an offense which comes off the fast break when the team doesn't score on the first attempt. This means that I expect the team to try to get more baskets from a high percentage area by bringing as quickly as possible to the offense more players than the defense. The secondary break (or early break) is then put into action. These are very quick plays and are directly generated by the fast break.

During the course of a regular pro season that I spent with the 76ers, the team was averaging 30 fast breaks a game. But during the playoffs this average dropped considerably to less than 20 breaks a game. Playoff time, of course, is like war, and the defense goes all out to stop movement. So in order to counteract this and get some more points from our fast break, we then started to stress and work on the latter part of our fast break. We worked hard in practice and the result was favorable. We obtained better shot selection even with the toughened defense.

One play that we utilized quite often was to go to our best offensive player (Julius Erving) after a made basket by the opponent, developing what we called a sideline break. The defense is beaten with a regular fast break and the ball is given to the top offensive player who is stationed in the low post area, the most difficult area on the court to defend. Here's how the play works:

Sideline Fast Break: Diagram 1-11. The center, 05, makes a pass to 01, the point guard, who dribbles and passes to 02. 03 posts down in the lane, while 05 screens for 04.

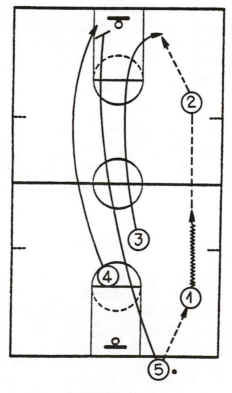

DIAGRAM 1-11

30

Another option is for a guard to push the ball upcourt, while the big guard and small forward make diagonal cuts, heading to the corners. The point guard will look for one of them for a quick shot.

THE CURL

Sometimes during a game you need to get the ball to certain players, your best shooter or a player who has a particularly hot hand. To bring this about effectively a "curl" is used to isolate that player. The curl can also become part of your regular offensive pattern. The purpose of the play is to clear out part of the floor and free the player used in the curl. Curling around a player positioned in the low post area creates a big problem for the defensive man: circling tightly around a low post frees a guard or forward, but also prevents the defensive man on the post from contesting the pass. If he does try and contest the pass, the post man is then left open for a pass.

Curl: Diagram 1-12. 01 has the ball and goes in the direction of the low post. 03 curls around 05, while 02 receives a screen from 04. 01 can pass to 03 or 05.

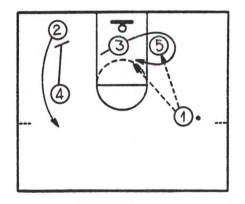

DIAGRAM 1-12

POSTING IN THE LANE

Pro players are masters in devising ways to post up in the lane, a place where it becomes almost impossible to defend. With the ball in the middle of the floor, the player waits in the lane and posts up directly under the basket, using the front of the rim as the target. Once he's allowed in this position by the defense, there's really nothing the defense can do; the man behind the offensive player can't jump to block a shot because of the rim. For this reason the play is generally effective.

Posting in the Lane: Diagram 1-13. 01 dribbles in the right wing area. This is the signal for 05 to step out and screen for 03. On the other side of the court, 04 makes a cut in the lane and goes in the low post area. 02 goes down.

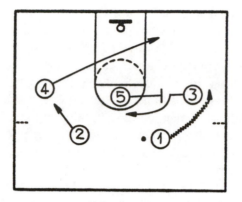

DIAGRAM 1-13

Posting in the Lane: Diagram 1-14. 01 passes the ball to 03, who can now hit 04 in the lane.

Posting in the Lane: Diagram 1-15. 01 passes the ball to 02 and goes in the corner, while 04 makes a pick for 03.

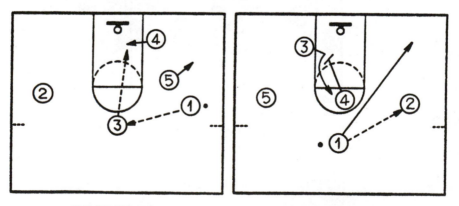

DIAGRAM 1-14   DIAGRAM 1-15

Posting in the Lane: Diagram 1-16. 02 passes the ball to 03 in the high post area. This player can now give it to 04 in the low post.

32

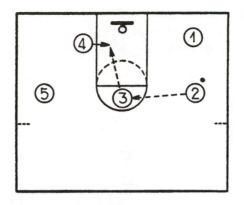

DIAGRAM 1-16

SCREEN THE SCREENER

One of the most effective plays in the pro game today is called "screen the screener" (sometimes also called "pick the picker"). Basically, the play calls for a screen for the player who previously had made a screen. This maneuver is very effective because the defensive man guarding the player who screened, generally never sees the new screen coming. Pro teams have adopted this play and there are many different ways to set it up. Here are three of them:

Screen the Screener: Diagram 1-17. 01 dribbles in the wing area and gives the ball to 04. 03 steps out and makes a blind pick for 01, who cuts in the lane and makes a pick for 05.

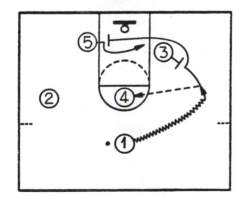

DIAGRAM 1-17

Screen the Screener: Diagram 1-18. 04 passes the ball to 03 and makes a screen for 01 in the lane. 01 comes high and receives a pass from 03. It's important on the screen for the screener to have as his target the lead hip of the defensive man.

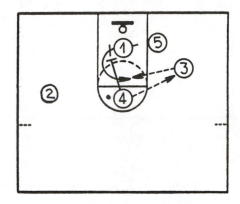

DIAGRAM 1-18

Screen the Screener: Diagram 1-19. This is another way to screen the screener. 01 is dribbling at the free-throw line extension. 05 screens for 03 and then receives a pick from 04. 01 gives the ball to 05 in the high post area.

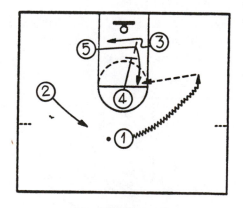

DIAGRAM 1-19

THE LOB PASS

Due to the great jumping ability of the pro players, many teams have incorporated the lob pass into their offensive arsenal. It can be a very powerful and morally devastating play, especially when the defense isn't expecting it.

Lob Pass: Diagram 1-20. 01 passes to 04 at the angle of the lane. 02 cuts on him and goes low while 03 cuts on 05. After 04 receives the ball, 05 makes a screen for 01, who then gets the ball.

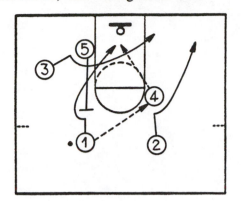

DIAGRAM 1-20

PLAYBACK

1) The offensive game is changing and reaching new levels of sophistication.

2) Coaches must now have a quick offense that comes off the unsuccessful fast break.

3) The "Curl" is a method of getting the ball to the player with the hot hand.

4) "Posting the Lane"—a tough situation for the defense.

5) "Screening the Screener"—one of the most effective new offenses.

6) Taking advantage of jumping ability—"The Lob Pass."

Offense

THE MAN-TO-MAN SET OFFENSE

by Dick Motta

Dick Motta, voted NBA coach of the Year (1970–71) with the Chicago Bulls (50-31) and coach of the NBA Champion Washington Bullets (1977–78), never played high school or college basketball. The first pro game he ever saw was the one he coached in Chicago in 1968. Nonetheless, Motta is one of the winningest coaches in NBA history.

After six years at Weber State University (1962–68) and three Big Sky titles, Motta took over the NBA Chicago Bulls in 1968. His team won the Midwest Division title in 1974–75. After four years as coach of the Washington Bullets (1976–80), Motta began coaching the expansion team Dallas Mavericks in 1980. In 1985, Motta guided Dallas to its second playoff berth, which capped the team's most successful season in its history.

I've always been a great believer in the set offense because it gives me virtually complete control over what's going on out on the court. By having this control, I find that I can move the players around whenever I need to or whenever a defensive setup dictates. This also gives me, as coach, the chance to take advantage of the unique offensive abilities of each of my players. If one player is hot, for example, I can call the plays from the bench to go to him. Conversely, when a player has an off-night, I'm able to run the plays away from him if need be.

Everyone likes to say that the pro basketball player, especially the superstar, has a fragile ego and cannot accept having a coach call the plays. My experience with my players is nothing like this. They seem to respond well to me calling the offense because it takes all the mystery out of the game; there will be no surprise when they come down and set up. Each player will know what will be happening and what his teammates will be doing.

I call my set offense "audio" because I either call or signal the plays. With this offense, numbers are called out, one through five. The numbers are never higher than five because I want the players to be able to signal the play with one hand.

My plays are 2, 3, 4 or 5 "up" when the hand is held up. They are 2, 3, 4, or 5 "down" when the hand is positioned towards the floor.

The number 1 play is only used for last-second shot situations.

The players: 01-02—guards
03-04—forwards
05   —center

"2 UP" PLAY

"2 Up" Play: Diagram 2-1. 01 has the ball, 03 and 05 make a double screen while 04 is in a low post position. 02 cuts in the middle, and if the defensive man follows him, he makes a "curl" around the double pick and then cuts in the lane and comes out of the pick of 04. 01 can hit 02 on the "curl" or when 02 is coming out of the lane around the pick of 04.

"2 Up" Play: Diagram 2-2. After the cut by 02, 05 sets down a screen for 03, who pops out. If 01 cannot pass to 02, he can give the ball to 03, coming off the screen.

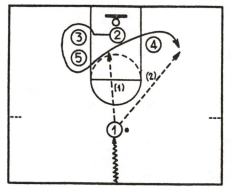

DIAGRAM 2-1   DIAGRAM 2-2

"2 Up" Play: Diagram 2-3. If 03, who has received the ball from 01, is not open for the shot, he makes what I call a "dump." He simply passes the ball down to 05, who is in the low post area.

"2 Up" Play: Diagram 2-4. Many times the defensive man stays high over the double pick, awaiting the offensive player who comes out of the lane. In this situation, 02 has two options: he can come out close to the baseline, a move called "pop out," or he can come back, using the pick of 04, a move I call "peek-a-boo."

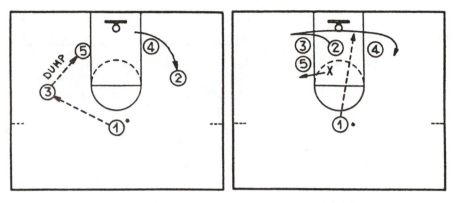

DIAGRAM 2-3   DIAGRAM 2-4

"3 UP" PLAY

"3 Up" Play: Diagram 2-5. We can start the play on both sides of the floor. Before the point guard crosses the half court, he calls out the signal in order to give the baseline players sufficient time to set up. After giving the ball to 03, 01 cuts in the lane. At the same time as the pass to 01, 02 fakes a cut-away and then makes a cut, using 05 as a screen (he can receive a lob pass here), and then posts up in the low post position. After the cut by 02, 05 comes to the ball and receives a pass from 03. The first option of 05 is to pass the ball to 02. In the meantime, 04 sets a low screen to 01.

"3 Up" Play: Diagram 2-6. After passing the ball to 05, 03 moves down and screens 02. 05 has three other passing options: (a) he can hit 02 on what I called a "jam"; (b) he can pass to 01, who comes out of the pick by 04; (c) he can give the ball to 03, who rolls toward the ball, after making the screen. Naturally, 05 can also shoot himself if he is open.

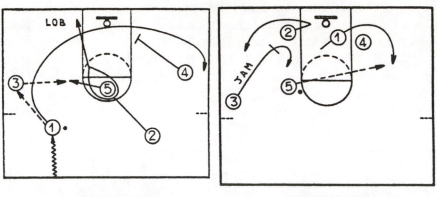

DIAGRAM 2-5　　　　　　　　　　　DIAGRAM 2-6

"3 Up" Play: Diagram 2-7. This is an excellent play to use when you have a tall guard who is being defended by a smaller man. In this case, 01 passes the ball to 02, cuts across the lane using 05 as the screen, and then posts up, while the other players make the same movements already seen before: 02 passes the ball to 04, cuts and clears out, and receives a pick from 03. At the same time, 05 goes to meet the ball or 04 passes the ball to 01 or 02.

"3 Up" Play: Diagram 2-8. 04 gives the ball to 05 and sets a screen down, a "jam" screen for 01. The purpose of this screen is to force the small defensive player to switch to 04, a taller forward.

"3 Up" Play: Diagram 2-9. In this situation, we have 04, the screener, the big man, and a guard being defended by a smaller player. 05 gives the ball to 01, who looks to give the ball to 04 in a low post area, what we call "dumping down low."

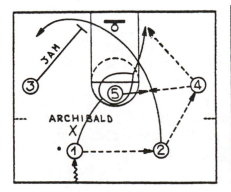

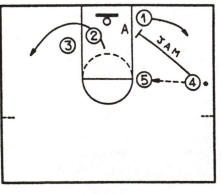

DIAGRAM 2-7　　　　　　　　　　　DIAGRAM 2-8

"4 UP" PLAY

"4 Up" Play: Diagram 2-10. This is a very popular and beneficial play, called "screen the screener." I like this play also because there is no ball handling involved which decreases the possibility of losing the ball. 01 dribbles until the free-throw line extension as quickly as possible. If 04 is guarded from behind, 01 can pass the ball directly to him in a position where he can play one-on-one.

"4 Up" Play: Diagram 2-11. If 04 is guarded in front and cannot receive the ball, he sets a screen on baseline for 03, who replaces 04. When 05 sees the screen of 04 for 03, he waits for one second and then makes a screen on the lane for 04: this is the action called "screen the screener."

"4 Up" Play: Diagram 2-12. The player with the ball, 01, has two options: he can hit 03 in the low post position or he can pass the ball to 04, who then receives a screen from 05.

"4 Up" Play: Diagram 2-13. If it is impossible to make one of the two passes, 01 changes side to the ball passing it to 02, who is coming to the center of the court. 02 dribbles on the left side to find a good passing angle and gives the ball to 05 in the low post area.

"4 Up" Play: Diagram 2-14. If 04 is guarded in front, we have another movement, with the same disposition seen before. While 01 dribbles toward the free-throw line extension, 04 makes what I call a "flair" cut. He comes high, using the screen of 05, and receives the ball from 01. One second after the cut of 04, 03 makes a "seal" cut on the baseline.

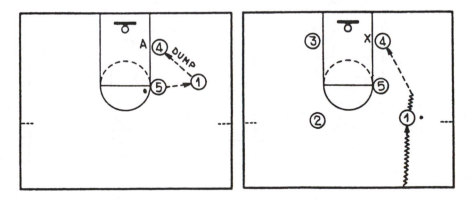

DIAGRAM 2-9   DIAGRAM 2-10

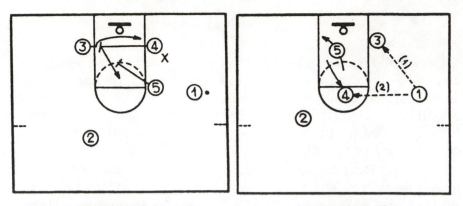

DIAGRAM 2-11   **DIAGRAM 2-12**

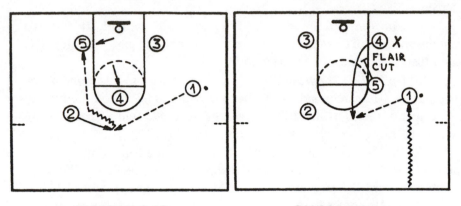

DIAGRAM 2-13   **DIAGRAM 2-14**

"4 Up" Play: Diagram 2-15. 04 can pass the ball to 03 or he can give the ball back to 01. 01 passes it to 05, who has taken a low post position after screening for 04.

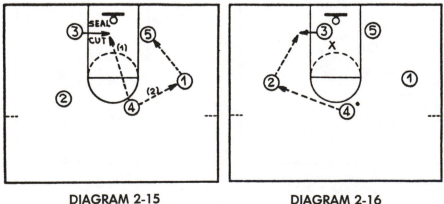

DIAGRAM 2-15   **DIAGRAM 2-16**

"4 Up" Play: Diagram 2-16. The first option of 04 is to hit 03 in the lane. But if 03 cannot receive the ball because the defensive man is between him and the ball, he makes a reverse cut and returns quickly to the initial position. 04 gives the ball to 02, who hit 03 in the low post position.

PLAYBACK

1. A set offense gives the coach control over his players and offensive movement.
2. With a coach calling the offensive sets from the bench, the mystery and surprise is taken out of the game for the players. Most players will respond well to this type of coaching.

STRUCTURING A MAN-TO-MAN ATTACK: "OUT SERIES OFFENSE"

by Jack McKinney

Jack McKinney, born July 13, 1935, spent 16 years as a high school and college coach, including eight seasons as head coach of his alma mater, St. Joseph's University (1965–74) in Philadelphia.

McKinney was named "Eastern College Coach of the Year" in 1974. He compiled a 165-83 record (.665) at St. Joe's before moving to the NBA in 1974. McKinney was head coach of the Los Angeles Lakers, and in 1980 became the head coach of the Indiana Pacers. In 1981, he was named NBA Coach of the Year. Jack retired last season.

Before adopting an offensive system, it must be well thought out in advance. Although it may seemingly work well for another team, you have to see if it will function as reliably with your own personnel. Most importantly, it has to be an easily productive offense.

The offensive setup which will be described here has been extremely effective for teams that I have been associated with. Of course, having an offensive-minded center who can also pass will certainly increase the effectiveness of this particular offense.

I was introduced to the "Out Series Offense" by Jack Ramsay when he coached the Buffalo Braves. His center at the time was Bob McAdoo, three-time NBA scoring champ. Ramsay took the offense with him to Portland where his center was Bill Walton, the NBA M.V.P. When I went to Los Angeles, I adapted it to the team there. Our center was the very talented Kareem Abdul-Jabbar, another NBA M.V.P. I continue to use this offense, even though at present I don't have a great center. This underscores the basic soundness and versatility of the offense. It's nice to note that with two of these teams that used the offense, Portland and Los Angeles, NBA Championships were the results.

This offense is designed to get everyone moving while at the same time offering every player a chance to express himself. The primary play which we run is called "1 Out." I call it "out" because it's easy to call a play by hollering 1, 2, 3, 4, or 5, with the fingers held *out* to signify the play.

The following is our "1 Out," with this numerical system used for clarification:

01—point guard or ballhandling guard

02—big or shooting guard

03—forward (along with 04)

05—center

"1 OUT" PLAY

"1 Out" isn't designed for a specific player. Essentially, it's a movement play which involves every player on the team.

"1 Out" Play: Diagram 2-17. 01 starts the play with a pass to either forward 03 or 04, then screens down for the opposite forward, 04 in this case, who comes to the circle area. Then 01 clears out away from the ball. 03, who has received the pass, looks for his own shot or drive. He can

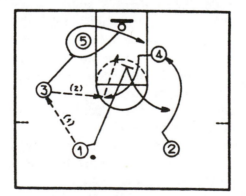

DIAGRAM 2-17

48

then pass to 04, who comes to the top of the circle. After the pass, 03 "slices off" 05, either at the top or bottom, looking for a pass from 04. Meanwhile, 02 is going down.

"1 Out" Play: Diagram 2-18. After the "slice" or "ruboff," 05 steps out, receives a pass from 04, and faces the basket. After looking for his own shot, 05 has different options in this order:

a) pass to 02 as baseline cutter off 03

b) pass to 01, as lane cutter off 04

c) pass to 03, getting the pick from 04 and coming to the top

"1 Out" Play: Diagram 2-19. After passing to 03, 05 screens away for 02 as lane cutter and for 01 as pop-out man. If 01 cannot shoot, a simple post up by 05 concludes the play.

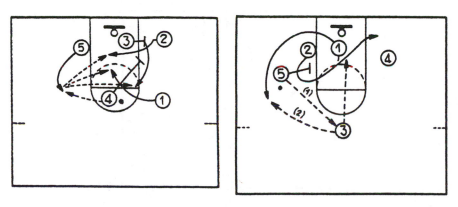

DIAGRAM 2-18   DIAGRAM 2-19

"2 OUT" PLAY

"2 Out" Play: Diagram 2-20. This play is specifically designed for the shooting guard. The play starts and looks like the "1 Out" (see Diagram 2-17). After 04 passes to 05, he goes down and forms a double screen with 03. 02 starts his baseline cutoff as he did in the "1 Out" play, but then comes back behind the screen of 03 and 04. 05 fakes a baseline pass to 02 then gives the ball to 01 at the top of the key. 01 looks to hit 02 coming behind the double screen.

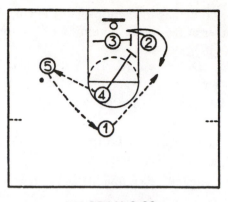

DIAGRAM 2-20

"2 Out" Play: Diagram 2-22. If 02 isn't open, 01 plays two-on-two with 05 who makes a pick-and-roll.

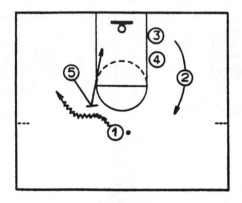

DIAGRAM 2-21

"3 OUT" PLAY

"3 Out" Play: Diagram 2-22. We use this play specifically for the forward, 03. The position of the players and the start is the same as "1 Out." After "slicing" off 05, 03 makes a reverse cut. 05, after the cut of 03, pops out, receives the ball from 04, and passes to 03.

"3 Out" Play: Diagram 2-23. 04, after passing the ball, makes a double screen with 01 for 02, who fakes to go in the lane, and then goes high and receives the ball from 05.

50

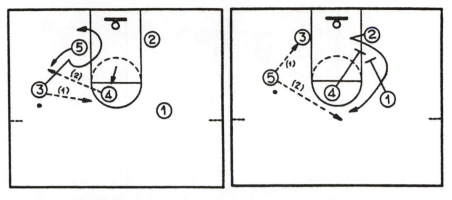

DIAGRAM 2-22   DIAGRAM 2-23

"3 Out" Play: Diagram 2-24. 05 gives the ball to 02 and then makes a pick for 03. If 02 can't shoot, he passes the ball to either 03 or 01, who pops out, or to 05 or 04 who posts up.

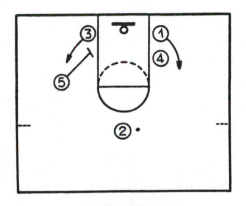

DIAGRAM 2-24

"4 OUT" PLAY

"4 Out" Play: Diagram 2-25. The beginning is the same as usual. This is simply a one-on-one opportunity for any player you designate. We want to clear out one side of the court to leave one player to play one-on-one. 01 gives the ball to 03 and then cuts in the lane and screens for 04. 03 gives the ball to 04, who comes high, and then "slices" off 05, circling back to the left, while 02 makes a cut on the baseline and comes high.

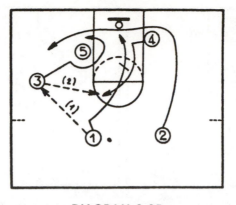

DIAGRAM 2-25

"4 Out" *Play: Diagram 2-26.* After the screen for 04, 01 makes a cut in the lane and comes out to the left, behind the screen of 03 and 05. In this way, we cleared out for the one-on-one of 04 on the right side of the lane.

"4 Out" *Play: Diagram 2-27.* If 04 can't shoot he stops near the basket and looks for the pass to 05, who comes up to the free throw line. Usually 05 is open because his defensive man helps on 04, who is driving to the basket.

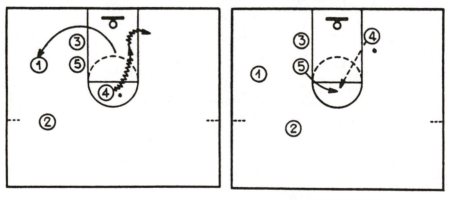

DIAGRAM 2-26   DIAGRAM 2-27

"5 OUT" PLAY

"5 Out" *Play: Diagram 2-28.* We run this play for the center, 05. The start is the same as "1 Out." 01 gives the ball to 03 and cuts. 03 passes to 04, who comes high, and then "slices" off 05, while 02 makes his usual baseline cut.

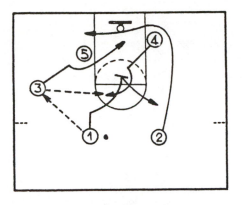

DIAGRAM 2-28

"5 Out" Play: Diagram 2-29. 04 immediately changes sides to the ball passing to 01, and then screens down for 05, who receives the pass from 01 and takes a jump shot.

"5 Out" Play: Diagram 2-30. If 05 isn't open for a shot, he continues his cut. After screening for 05, 04 makes another pick for 02, who comes high and receives a pass for 01.

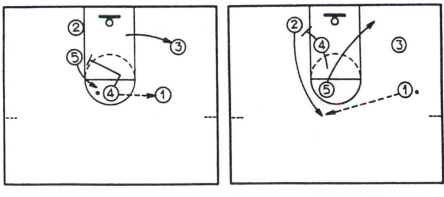

DIAGRAM 2-29   DIAGRAM 2-30

PLAYBACK

1) Before finally adopting an offensive system for your team, you have to know your personnel and be sure they have the capabilities for proper execution. An offense must be easily productive.

2) The "Out Series" works especially well for a team with an offensive, passing-minded center.

THE SONICS OFFENSE

by Lenny Wilkens

In January, 1982 44-year-old Lenny Wilkens, coach of the Seattle Supersonics, became the youngest NBA coach ever to notch up 400 career victories. Wilkens, now in his twelfth season of coaching in the NBA, first with Portland and since 1977 with Seattle, has racked up impressive seasons. In 1978–79, his Seattle Supersonics won the NBA World Championship.

Wilkens, a nine-time NBA All Star, and MVP in the 1971 game, has an overall coaching record of .528, one of the best records of all NBA coaches. He is now General Manager of the Sonics.

I prefer to play the transition game because my teams seem to play more effectively with the fast break (what we call "early offense") than with a slow down or half court game. My players seem to get their maximum offensive punch from playing on the open court.

To best utilize this type of offense, you need players who are great runners. They must be able to pass the ball exceptionally well to the open man. Having a quick and creative point guard is also a must.

I want my team to go for the fast break at every opportunity. Knowing, of course, that they won't score on each try, I have incorporated early offense into our plays. These are quick-hitting plays that come directly from the fast break and involve all five players.

FAST BREAK AFTER A FREE THROW

Fast Break After a Free Throw: Diagram 2-31. When the opposing team is at the free throw line, we put the two big men, 04 and 05, down

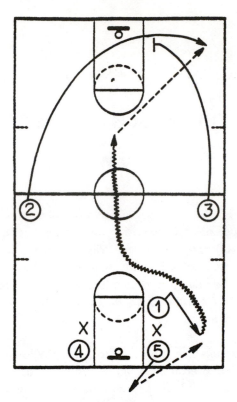

DIAGRAM 2-31

on the lane for the rebound. The point guard, 01, at the right side of the three seconds area, is in a position where he can: (1) block out the shooter, and above all (2) receive the first pass off the fast break. The other two players, 02 and 03, are near the midcourt line. If we take the rebound, or in case the shot is made, 05 takes the ball and passes it to 01 as quickly as possible. If the defense tries to pressure 01, the receiver of the outlet pass, 04, makes a screen to free him.

The first option of 01, who has dribbled to the middle of the court, is to pass the ball to 02 (our shooting guard), who then cuts down in the lane and gets a screen from 03.

If the defense changes, 01 can pass the ball to 03, who steps in the lane. Sometimes the defense tries to push 01, the man with the ball, in the opposite direction of the pick. In this case, 02 will make a pick for 03.

EARLY OFFENSE

If we can't score with a fast break we'll then run our early offense, taking advantage of the formation we have at the end of a fast break.

Early Offense: Diagram 2-32. If nothing happens from the fast break, we have 03 in a low post position, 02 in the wing area, 01 outside the circle, 04 on the other side, and 05 on the left wing area. 01 passes the ball to 02.

Early Offense: Diagram 2-33. From this formation we can immediately start our early offense without any delay, hopefully beating a not completely set defense. 02 gives the ball back to 01, who passes it to 04. At the same time 03 steps out and makes a blind pick for 02. This player cuts in the lane and can receive a pass from 04. Now 01 makes a pick for 03 (pick the picker) and then steps out in the corner. 04 can now hit 02, who cuts in the lane, 05, or 03.

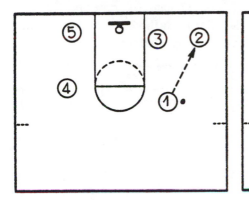

DIAGRAM 2-32

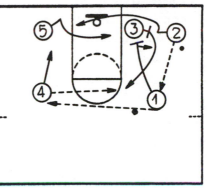

DIAGRAM 2-33

Early Offense: Diagram 2-34. 04 gives the ball to 03 and then goes low to screen for 02 who is cutting in the lane and then steps out. 03 can pass the ball to 02 or 05. In this offense we have all five players involved and moving around the lane, preventing the defense from setting up.

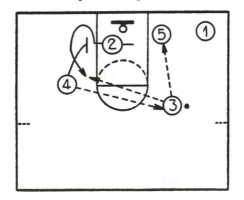

DIAGRAM 2-34

57

THE SET OFFENSE

If we can't score with the early offense, we move to the set offense. The following is a set play we use quite often because it's very effective with the type of players we have on our team.

Set Offense: Diagram 2-35. 05 comes out and makes a pick for 03 who cuts in the three seconds area. He then goes in the high post area and receives the ball from 01.

Set Offense: Diagram 2-36. After 03 has received the ball, 01 and 02 make a cross cut (we have a rule that the passer always cuts first). At the same time 04 and 05 screen down. If the defense stays higher than the screeners, 03 can give the ball to 01 or 02 near the baseline. If the defensive men stay with them, 01 and 02 run in the lane, each of them going to the opposite side of the court to get the ball.

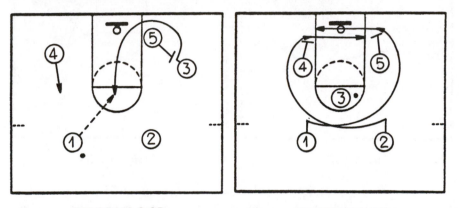

DIAGRAM 2-35   DIAGRAM 2-36

Set Offense: Diagram 2-37. When the cutters come out of the lane, 04 and 05 open themselves to the ball, getting in position to receive a pass from 03.

Set Offense: Diagram 2-38. If the occasion exists, we'll go to two-on-two play. We can create more potential scoring opportunities this way. 03 gives the ball to 01 and then sets a screen. 01 tries to penetrate and will then have different options:

a) he can shoot

b) pass to 02, who goes down

c) pass to 03 who stepped out after the screen

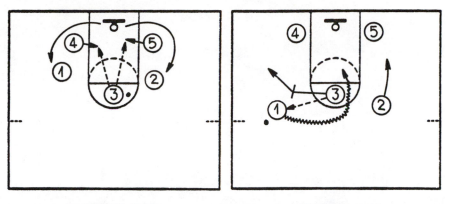

DIAGRAM 2-37 **DIAGRAM 2-38**

PLAYBACK

1) Determine whether the fast break or "early offense" suits your team.
2) The key to this determination is whether you have superior runners who can move the ball and pass it quickly as well.
3) If so, go for the fast break every opportunity.
4) Back up the break with your "early offense."

Defense

BASIC MAN-TO-MAN HALF-COURT DEFENSE

by Jack Ramsay

Jack Ramsay graduated from St. Joseph's (Philadelphia) in 1949 where he captained the basketball team in his senior year. From 1955 to 1966, with Ramsay as head coach, St. Joe's went to 10 post-season tournaments.

After head coaching stints with the Philadelphia 76ers (1968-72), Buffalo (1972–76), Jack Ramsay settled in with the Portland TrailBlazers. Since then Ramsay has guided the Blazers to the playoffs all but one season. His 1976–77 squad had a regular season record of 49-33 (.598) and went on to win the NBA Championship.

Defense has always played a very important role for all the teams I have coached at college level when I was at St. Joe's, as well as the pro level. Defense is extremely important at whatever level you coach. It's the base upon which you'll build a winning team. Basketball has a great many examples of defenses aiding in victory. UCLA in the John Wooden era was built on Wooden's defensive emphases. The Boston Celtics were able to win so many games under Red Auerbach because of the emphasis that was put on playing "D."

When I speak of defense I don't mean a passive style of play. I'm not talking of players putting on the pressure in the final two minutes of the game, racing all over the court in a desperate attempt to keep the other team from scoring. The style that I'm speaking about is tough, aggressive, and attacking, played from opening tipoff to the final buzzer. The entire time the defense is pushing the other team to make mistakes, to give up the ball. They don't *wait* for the mistakes of the offense, the defense *causes* them.

To play such an intensive and demanding defense, you—the coach—must physically prepare the players for the battles of the season. They have to be in shape to go all out, every game, all season long. Your defense will dictate the tempo of the game, putting both physical and mental pressure on the offense. In playing this hardnosed style of ball, I push my players to do different things: they play hard on the ball, contesting both first and second passes. They push the ball away from the basket and harass every offensive movement.

I divide defense into eight distinct phases. They are:

1) The first step is to put a lot of pressure on the player with the ball. We want to stop the dribbler from bringing the ball up on defense. We want to contest the first pass coming off their pattern.

2) We want to avoid being beaten by the long pass which will bring easy baskets.

3) We want to stop every organized fast break.

4) We have to undo the effectiveness of offensive screens.

5) It's a must to contest every pass to the high and low post areas.

6) At all times we want to prevent a player from going one-on-one.

7) All cuts and all passes must be contested.

8) Each player must block out.

If you are able to control these eight basic phases of the game, you're on the way to having a winning team.

DEFENSIVE STANCE

Defense begins with the basic stance. The player must be willing to bend over. The weight of the body should be evenly distributed on both feet. The hand on the side of the forward foot should be extended and open (palm upward) to harass every movement of the dribbler. The other hand must be used to stop the pass and crossover dribble.

If the defender is guarding a player close to the ball, he will extend the arm and the leg nearest to the ball, touching the body of the offensive player with the other arm. From this position we create problems of ball circulation.

A player who plays on the "help side" of the court forms a triangle with two of his teammates. He must remain in a position to see both the ball and his man.

The farther away the offensive man is from the ball, the farther away the defensive player will be from him. However, the defensive man should always be in a position to reach out quickly and snare the ball.

I always tell my players who guard the dribbler to push him and make him do reverse dribbles. Crossover dribbles in front of defenders are situations that I don't want.

The following basic drill, called "mirror movement," is an effective way to teach your players defensive stance and proper movement. The entire team should spread out on the court. They should make the same movements in four directions as dictated either by the coach or a teammate standing in front of them. The length of the drill is 1 minute, 50 seconds. Rest 10 seconds and repeat again. We usually work on this drill at every practice.

FIRST DEFENSIVE PHASE

The first step in building sound defensive play is to teach your players defensive stance. It's important to note that we don't move backwards, a usual defensive reaction you see so much today. What I want is lateral movement. This way penetration to the basket will be prevented. It's a mistake for a defensive player to back up because it gives the offensive player space to move, an advantage that could mean the difference between winning and losing. It's important that the defender study the player in front of him. He must decide which part of the court he should pressure him in, figure out which hand he favors when he dribbles.

Zig-Zag Drill: Diagram 3-1. This drill stresses strong defensive pressure on the dribbler. We pair one offensive player, 01, and one defensive player, X1. X1 must try to force 01 to reverse his dribble, try to steal the ball, and if beaten, recuperate. Stress must be put on keeping good defensive stance throughout the drill.

The reaction drill will teach proper movement against dribblers. Put offensive and defensive couples on the floor. The drill starts with a fake by the offensive player to which the defense has to respond.

Reaction Drill: Diagram 3-2. Two lines of players, one on defense and the other on offense, take the court. After a fake, 01 receives the ball from X1 and tries different ways to get by. He may fake a drive, take a

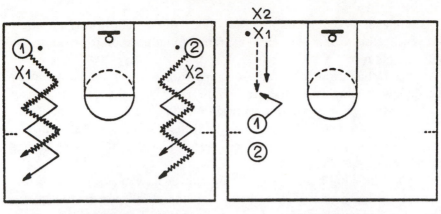

DIAGRAM 3-1   DIAGRAM 3-2

shot, or make a pass before settling in for one-on-one. The drill is repeated by guards, forwards, and centers.

SECOND DEFENSIVE PHASE

As mentioned before, I don't want to give up easy baskets. We try to stop all long passes after the rebound. To do this, the three big men have to go in for the offensive rebound. This will give us a better opportunity under the boards to score off the rebound. If a basket is made, we pressure the possible receiver of the outlet pass with the guard who was moving our offensive pattern. The other guard, not directly involved in the offense, hustles back to our defensive half court.

THIRD DEFENSIVE PHASE

Stopping the long pass doesn't mean we have stopped the fast break. With the following drill, we try to stop the organized fast break.

Stopping the Fast Break: Diagram 3-3. The coach, at the free-throw line, shoots the ball. Two rebounders go to the boards, take the rebound, and make the outlet pass. X1 and X2 try to pressure the rebounders. When the outlet pass is made, X3 and X4 will run as quickly as possible back on defense.

If a player encounters a two-on-one situation, he must begin his defense at the three seconds area. Easy lay-ups must be prevented here.

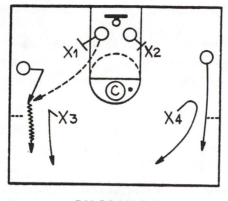

DIAGRAM 3-3

FOURTH DEFENSIVE PHASE

The pick-and-roll, as well as different types of screens, are common in all the offensive patterns used today. It, therefore, becomes very important to work hard against all these stratagems. It's very important for defensive players to call out to each other as they work around and through screens and picks. They have to tell each other which side a screen is coming from, and how close they are from the screeners. This verbal communication is the very base of a sound defense.

Lateral Screen: Diagram 3-4. On this type of screen, the defensive player screened, X1, can slide over the screen. Normally this is the best solution. He may also go behind the screen if the screen is away from the

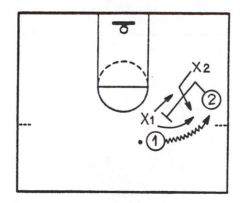

DIAGRAM 3-4

67

basket, always with the help of X2. He may also go through the middle if possible.

Horizontal Screen: Diagram 3-5. If the offense makes a horizontal screen between two players of equal height, we systematically change in order to keep maximum pressure on the ball. We may also be able to pick up a charge.

Vertical Screen: Diagram 3-6. In this case, the defender of the screener must open up and face the dribbler. This will close the penetration. By doing this he will also provide time for his teammates to recuperate without making defensive changes.

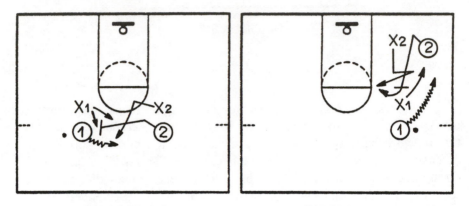

DIAGRAM 3-5   **DIAGRAM 3-6**

Multiple Screen Drill: Diagram 3-7. Each day at practice we run this drill. 01 gives the ball to 02 and makes a shuffle cut on 03, and then makes a vertical screen for 02. We have different game situations such as

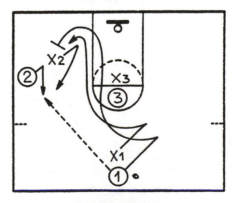

DIAGRAM 3-7

68

the give-and-go, blind picks, and vertical screens coming out of this drill. The three defensive players, X1, X2, and X3, work against these moves.

FIFTH DEFENSIVE PHASE

One of the most dangerous spots for defense is in the high and low post areas. The ball is very close to the basket and can easily be swung around on both sides of the court. For this reason we work hard to eliminate the effectiveness of screens made within the three seconds area.

Blind Screen in the Lane Drill: Diagram 3-8. In this situation, we follow the principles seen before. X1 must stay above the screener, fronting the defensive man who is coming off the screen. He must then return immediately to his own offensive player while the teammate screened, X2, must quickly recover.

Contesting the Pass and the Cut Drill: Diagram 3-9. In this drill we put two offensive players, 01 and 02, in the low post position. Two defensive players, X1 and X2, will try and contest all passes and anticipate cuts. Two stationary players are used to pass the ball.

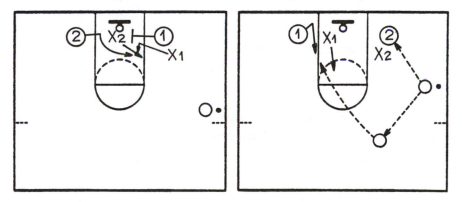

DIAGRAM 3-8   DIAGRAM 3-9

Double Pick Drill: Diagram 3-10. We defend in two different ways against the double pick. In part A of the diagram, X1 comes out to pick up 03 who is coming off the double screen. X2 and X3 go on 01 and 02. We move this way to avoid penetration. In part B of the diagram, X1 comes out to contest the pass to 03, who is coming off the double pick. This will allow time for X3 to recover and get his own man.

Shuffle Cut Drill: Diagram 3-11. In the NBA, cuts made off the high post are commonly called shuffle cuts. The following drill is effec-

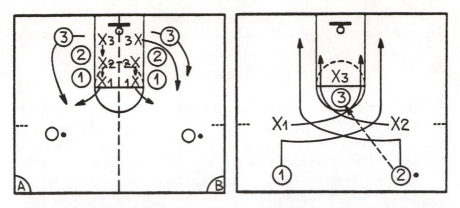

DIAGRAM 3-10   DIAGRAM 3-11

tive in teaching how to defend against them. Place two outside players, 01 and 02, and one inside player, 03, with their defenders. 02 passes the ball to 03 and then the outside players cut in the opposite direction. X1 and X2 must first of all go near the offensive post and then follow the assigned player. We make this move to avoid being beaten on the give-and-go. Normally we don't make any changes, but, if necessary, two men can change.

Cut on the Low Post Drill: Diagram 3-12. This is a good drill for the cut on the low post. When 02 gives the ball to 03, X2 doubles on the low post. If the low post player passes the ball outside to 01, X2 then goes on 01, while X1 goes on 02.

Pick for the Forward Drill: Diagram 3-13. Here is a good drill for three-on-three play with a pick for the forward made by the low post player. 02 receives the ball, and just before the pick gives the ball back to

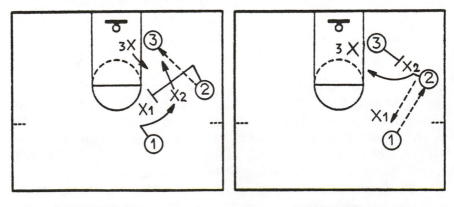

DIAGRAM 3-12   DIAGRAM 3-13

01. He cuts on the screen of 03. X2 and X3 have to work hard to avoid being beaten.

Four-on-Four Drill: Diagram 3-14. Two guards, 01 and 02, and two forwards, 03 and 04, take the floor with their defensive counterparts. The offense plays give-and-go, using cuts and screens. We have a standard rule in this drill that every offensive player must make two consecutive screens and that the offense can only score after three passes have been made.

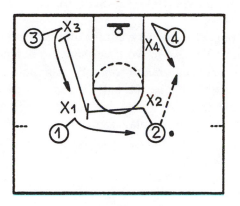

DIAGRAM 3-14

SIXTH DEFENSIVE PHASE

One-on-One Clear Cut Drill: Diagram 3-15. It's very common in the pro game to try and isolate the best player in a certain area and let him go one-on-one. For this reason we work very hard with this drill to

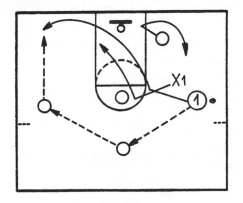

DIAGRAM 3-15

71

prevent this from happening. The defender must try and push the offensive player to different areas on the court, hopefully to a place where the shooter is less proficient. In this drill we have four stationary players, while 01 and X1 play one-on-one. 01 can use screens or different types of cuts and then try to isolate himself. X1 must contest him and keep him away from the basket.

SEVENTH DEFENSIVE PHASE

As I've mentioned, we don't want the offensive player to receive the ball near the basket. We have to work very hard to defend against all cuts made in the three seconds area. From my standpoint, if an offensive player cuts to the same side as the ball, I want the defensive player to open up towards the ball, being able to touch the body of the cutter with his arm. On the contrary, if the player cuts toward the ball from the help side, the defender must be very close to the offensive player, guarding him in front, face to face.

If a pass is made to the center, the outside players will float towards the center to help out, defending against all backdoor cuts.

EIGHTH DEFENSIVE PHASE

One of the most important aspects of the game of basketball is rebounding. Generally, the team that gets the most rebounds will be the eventual game winner. It's, therefore, imperative for all the players to block out on defense. Each player must make contact with his man when a shot is taken, staying low, eyes looking upward and watching the flight of the ball.

To build a tough, strong defense, a coach needs to sell his ideas to his players. The payoff isn't found in terms of celebrity status or lines in the sports pages. The players have to realize that it takes sacrifice and hard work, but defense will be the base upon which all of their victories originate.

PLAYBACK

1) Tough, aggressive, attacking defense that's played from opening tipoff to final buzzer can be as potent a weapon as the best offense.

2) Defense can be divided into eight phases:

    a) Pressure the ball.

    b) Avoid being beaten by the long pass.

    c) Stop all organized fast breaks.

    d) Break up screens.

    e) Contest all passes to the high and low post.

    f) Shut down all one-on-one play.

    g) Contest all cuts and passes, especially in the high post area.

    h) Block out after every shot.

TIMING AND THE USE OF FULL-COURT PRESSURE

by Rick Pitino

A 1974 graduate of the University of Massachusetts where he captained the basketball team, Rick Pitino went on to be an assistant coach at the University of Hawaii and Syracuse University.

In 1978, Pitino was named head coach at Boston University. During the next five years, he compiled an impressive 91-51 record before finally joining the New York Knicks as an assistant coach in 1983. He is now head coach of Providence College.

The basic premise behind matching up and applying full-court pressure on defense is to create a trap, causing the offense to move from their strong areas, and possibly give up the ball.

The match-up press can be a devastating weapon if it's well-executed. Not only will it cause many turnovers, but if and when turnovers are turned into baskets, the match-up press can be viewed as a formidable "offensive" weapon as well.

With this defensive setup as part of your game plan, emotions and intensity level will get very high on the court; the involvement of your bench is vital. Playing nine men is the real key here in obtaining maximum results. Because you're bound to have some weak defenders on the squad, you shouldn't be discouraged from making use of the press. Generally, a mistake on the part of the "weak link" will not cause you a basket in the backcourt area.

In practice sessions I like to work on the press because it's here that the team gets to know how it works and what the responsibilities of each player are. To work on it effectively, you should separate your team into a first and a second unit. It's essential and vital for a coach to accurately chart what goes on when the press is employed. An average of 20 deflections per game caused by the press is considered to be good.

Remember, a deflection doesn't always lead to a possession by the defense. But applied pressure will cause the offensive team to make mistakes. You, your assistant, or manager should chart the press in practices, and in the game by the quarter or half. Here is a hand reference to use when charting the press:

D-deflections
S-steal
T-tip from behind
F-foul
J-jump ball

By using the chart, you will quickly discover exactly how the press is helping your team. Based on these figures, you will then be able to make defensive changes based on fact rather than intuition.

CHARACTERISTICS OF THE MATCH-UP PRESS

a. The front will change according to the movements of the ball.
b. All players are played straight up and close, encouraging uncontrolled dribbling.
c. Four of the players will be playing with knees bent in the shortstop position, their hands raised up.
d. The dribbler must never get by the defender with one dribble. Two players are necessary for proper rotation into traps.
e. Play back into passing lanes if the center is used as a man in the middle of the ball reverse.
f. All defenders must retreat in a crouched, shortstop position when the off player vacates an area. He stops when the off man is seen (with peripheral vision).
g. Never play in front of an offensive man.

Diagram 3-16. We start this defense in the 2-2-1 basic formation: X1 and X2 are the guards, X3 and X4 are forwards, and X5 the center. We stay with the sideline entry and the man with the ball is covered straight up, but not too close; we want to encourage the dribble. We can

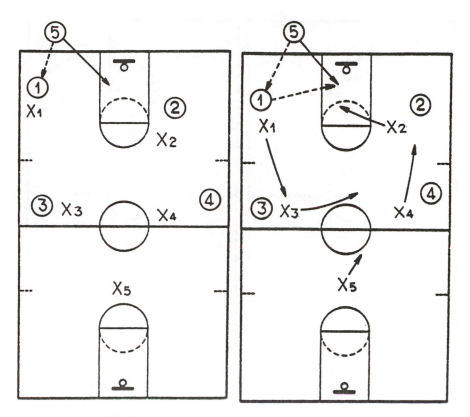

DIAGRAM 3-16   DIAGRAM 3-17

deny the inbound pass by matching up man-to-man with the center guarding the long pass.

Diagram 3-17. If 05 passes the ball to 01 and then he receives the pass back (the ball is now in the middle of the court), we change the defensive formation, rotating into a 1-3-1 alignment. If the opposing center is in the middle with the ball, the defense retreats back and we stay in the passing lanes. On the contrary, if the offensive player in the middle of the lane is *not* the center, we pressure him, still allowing him to dribble, encouraging a turnover.

Diagram 3-18. As shown here, we are now in a 1-3-1 formation with X2 at the top, X1 at the left wing, X3 in the middle, X4 at the right wing, and X5 as the last man on defense.

Diagram 3-19. If 01, the man with the ball, tries to dribble in the middle, both of the defensive guards have to move to him. X1 slides to the middle and we create a 1-3-1 alignment. The guard stays with the dribbler to create this alignment.

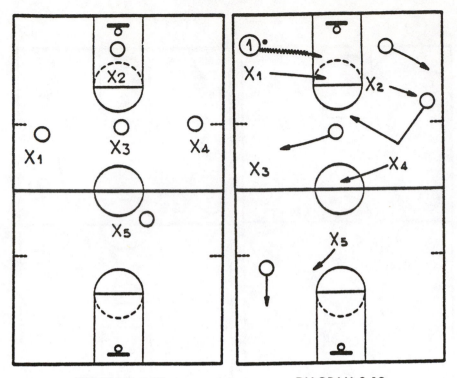

DIAGRAM 3-18   **DIAGRAM 3-19**

Diagram 3-20. If we decide to steal the inbound pass, we put a defensive man on the player who is in charge of the inbound pass. If the offense passes the ball to the sideline, we quickly rotate into our usual format, 2-2-1, moving from the 1-2-1-1 alignment.

ROTATION PRINCIPLES

Diagram 3-21. Anytime the player with the ball tries to dribble in the middle, we make a trap using X1, his defensive man, and X2, the opposite guard. If the dribbler beats the defender, one of them must try to tip the ball from behind. This part is critical. Anytime the first line of defense is beaten, the defensive player must chase the ball and try to *tip it forward*. A successful tip more often than not will result in a basket. Tipping from behind also aids in playing transition defense against the fast break.

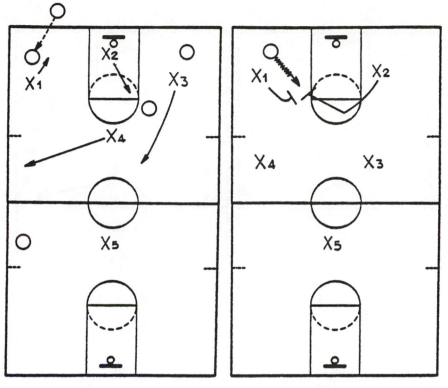

DIAGRAM 3-20   DIAGRAM 3-21

Diagram 3-22. Anytime the offensive player makes an uncontrolled dribble alongside the sideline, we trap aggressively with X1, the guard, and X3, the forward, while X5, the center, rotates on the ball side. In the meantime, X2, the other guard, goes in the middle for a couple of seconds, then gambles back for the reversal pass. X5 rotates on the ball side and X4 guards the long pass. A very aggressive trap such as this will force the offensive player to try and pass to the middle. If that is blocked, he will then look long. The other three defensive players must be alert to intercept all passes.

Diagram 3-23. If the first player who gets the ball can pass it in the middle, it's usually because the defensive player plays with his hands down and doesn't apply enough pressure. The team must then retreat to the passing lanes and encourage dribbling. X1 should try and tip the ball from behind and X4 has to stop any further penetration to the middle.

79

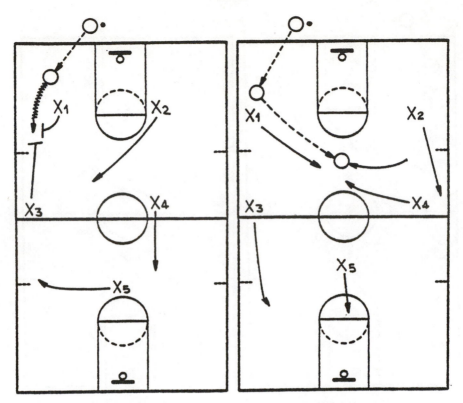

DIAGRAM 3-22   DIAGRAM 3-23

Diagram 3-24. If the ball is reversed quickly on the sideline, starting from the 1-3-1 alignment, we try to make a trap at half court. X1 and X2 make the trap, X3 guards the middle and is responsible for the reversal, X4 goes in the middle of the three seconds lane, and X5 plays just outside the lane on the ball side.

Diagram 3-25. If the offensive player trapped at midcourt passes the ball to the corner, X5 will trap with X2, who will run directly at the shooter trying to disturb his concentration. X4 goes toward the ball, X1 runs on the weakside lane, and X3 plays the middle passing lane.

Diagram 3-26. If the ball is reversed on some other part of the floor besides the middle, we stay with the 2-2-1 alignment. If X2 cannot place pressure on the ball because of a quick reversal, X4 goes up, and all the other players make a rotation opposing the ball. X5 will try and intercept the pass.

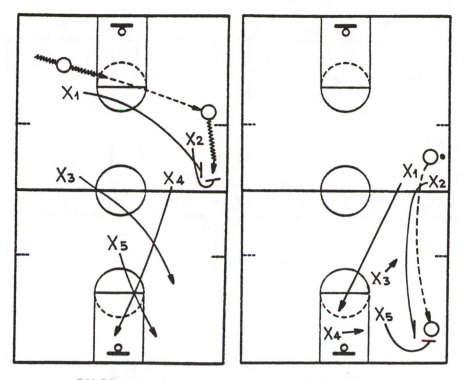

DIAGRAM 3-24   DIAGRAM 3-25

DRILLS FOR THE MATCH-UP PRESS

4×4×4 Drill: Diagram 3-27. This drill accomplishes many things both offensively and defensively. 0A, 0B, 0C, and 0D attack X1 and X2. When the ball passes the hash mark, X3 and X4 run on defense trying to break up the offensive advantage.

4×4×4 Drill: Diagram 3-28. On a missed shot, the four offensive players press in the backcourt against the X's. They stop to steal and defend at midcourt. If the defensive team steals the ball and scores, it plays a 2-2-1 match-up alignment, using the rotation of the match-up press. If the defense crosses the midcourt line, they will attack against 01 and 02 the same way as shown before.

Many offensive and defensive aspects of the game are worked on with this simple drill:

a. Developing fast break lanes, passing, and scoring

b. Defensive and offensive rebounding

81

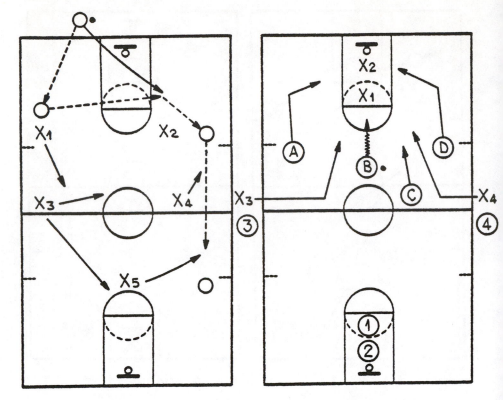

DIAGRAM 3-26   DIAGRAM 3-27

c. Jamming outlets—pitching out on a break

d. Trapping and stealing—passing against extreme pressure

e. Defensive anticipation—stopping the ball offensively

f. V cutting—tipping from behind

Note: When the offensive break is stopped and the defense plays four-on-four, offense runs motion.

THREE-MAN ZIGZAG DRILL

We put three defensive and three offensive players at half court. The offensive unit will use different alignments to make the inbound pass in an attempt to break the pressure. The defensive unit will learn how to trap from this drill.

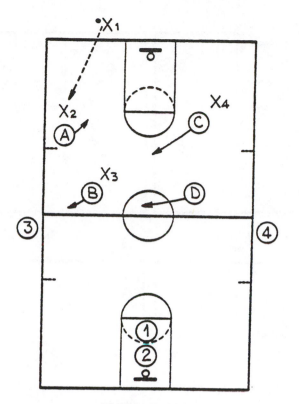

DIAGRAM 3-28

PRESS STATIONS

Denial Drill: Diagram 3-29. We put two defensive players, X1 and X2, on two offensive players, 01 and 02, while another player is used to inbound the ball only. The defensive men will call "change" every time the offensive players make a screen, and they will try to run and trap.

Trap-and-Split Drill: Diagram 3-30. There will be two pairs of offensive and defensive players on half court. X1 and X2 double-team the dribbler and then split if he makes a pass to the wing. The defense works in this drill on trying for deflections and containing the offensive man in as small a space as possible.

Anticipate-and-Steal Drill: Diagram 3-31. We position two players, X1 and X2, who must trap, and another, X3, who must anticipate the pass to one of the two wings. X1 and X2 must trap the dribbler when he drives

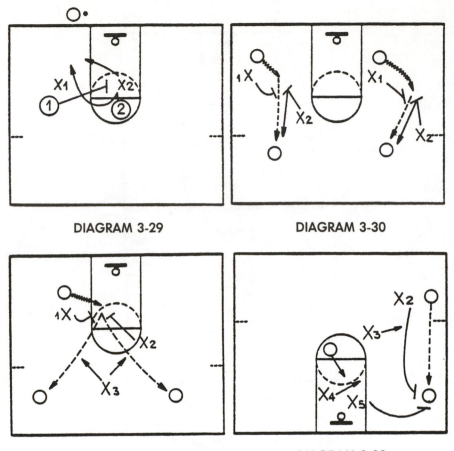

DIAGRAM 3-29

DIAGRAM 3-30

DIAGRAM 3-31

DIAGRAM 3-32

in the middle, while X3 tries to steal the pass to one of the two wings (staying in the crouched, shortstop position).

Corner-Trap and Rotation Drill: Diagram 3-32. Use two offensive men, one with the ball, the other in the corner. The drill begins with a pass to the corner. X2 runs at the shooter to trap, X5 comes out of the three seconds area to trap 02, while X4 anticipates a cut in the middle of the three seconds lane. X3 goes to the ball side to try and steal a return pass.

PLAYBACK

1) Being able to play at least nine men is the real key in obtaining maximum results with the full-court press.

2) An average of 20 deflections per game is considered good. Have some-one on the team chart the press by quarter or half.

3) Anytime the first line of defense is penetrated, have the defensive player chase the ball, trying to tip it forward.

A PRO'S EYE-VIEW OF THE ZONE

by Don Casey

During his nine years as Head Coach at Temple University, Don Casey chalked up an impressive 151-94 record (.616) with the Owls. Temple earned one NCAA bid and three NIT invitations during this span. Casey was twice honored as East Coast Conference Coach of the Year.

He currently is the Assistant Coach of the San Diego Clippers.

PHILOSOPHY

There are many coaches who think that the easy way out on defense is to play a zone. This is a mistake. Effective zone defense is hard work and will yield results. Hours of patient instruction by a coach is needed to implement a successful zone properly. Each player must come to understand his position and all of its ramifications.

Zones demand five-man choreographed movements. As the situation dictates, each player has to shift quickly, denying the good pass and offensive movement. This must be continually accomplished for any zone to be effective.

While zone slides can be taught relatively quickly, perfection is attained only through fundamental defensive skills coupled with sound unit zone drills.

LEAD-UP DRILLS

In order for the zone to be effective, individual defense must be taught and stressed. When guarding the ball in the zone, man-to-man principles are employed on the ball. While each coach has his favorite drills, the following have been successful for me:

ONE-ON-ONE SERIES

One-on-One Series: Diagram 3-33. The offensive player, 01, drives towards the top of the circle. When he reaches this position, he can make a crossover reverse dribble, shoot, or else continue the dribble for the lay-up. The offense should go at top speed trying to turn the corner and/or use a change-of-pace dribble en route to the top of the circle. The defensive player, X1, cannot try to steal the ball until the offensive player reaches the top of the circle. The drill can also be made on the other side of the court.

One-on-One Series: Diagram 3-34. The offensive player, 01, drives towards the corner, trying to turn the corner on the dribble, while the defensive player, X1, follows him. He can't attempt a steal until the offensive player turns the corner. However, if this isn't possible, 01 can roll, cross over, or reverse-dribble to proceed to the basket. X2 and 02 work this same drill on the other side of the court.

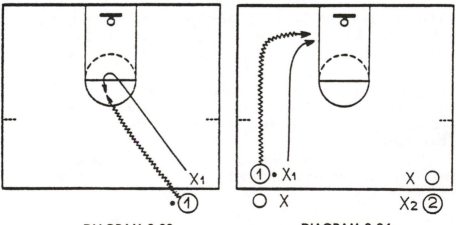

DIAGRAM 3-33   DIAGRAM 3-34

ONE-ON-ONE HALF COURT

One-on-One Half Court: Diagram 3-35. The players form three lines at half court, with one offensive and one defensive player. Each line has a ball. 01 drives toward the basket using various techniques to beat the defensive player, X1. The dribbler can't turn his back to the defense. By becoming more vulnerable, this puts more pressure on the offense and gives the defense a better chance at success. After the first couple has finished the drill, 02 and X2 do the same drill, followed by 03 and X3, each time on the right side of the basket. The drill can then be performed on the other side of the court. Upon completing the drill at the center and two sides of the court, offensive and defensive players switch positions. The coach can add restricted rules: limiting the type of shots allowed; jump shots, hooks, drives; or jump shots allowed only in the three seconds area.

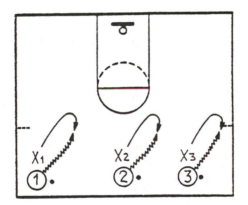

DIAGRAM 3-35

MEETING THE DRIBBLER

Meeting the Dribbler: Diagram 3-36. The defense, X1, is waiting for the dribbler, 01, who is coming up quickly, but under control. The defensive man can jam or force him to change direction, but not give up the uncontested shot. The coach may limit the offensive players, allowing them to take only jump shots for example. X1, when the action has

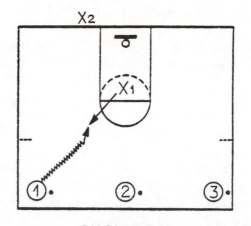

DIAGRAM 3-36

ended, retrieves the ball and goes to the line of 01. X2 quickly steps in to meet the dribbler and 01 becomes the next defensive player after X2 completes his turn.

MEETING THE SIDELINE DRIBBLER

Meeting the Sideline Dribbler: Diagram 3-37. Due to the fact that good offensive teams may try to penetrate zones by dribbling through them, we have to contain this type of movement. The defensive players, X1 and X2, have to "turn them" so the split won't be too harmful. However, to make this drill difficult for the offense, have them alternate when they can and cannot turn their backs to the defense. The offense should also vary its starting point. The drill is worked on both sides of the court.

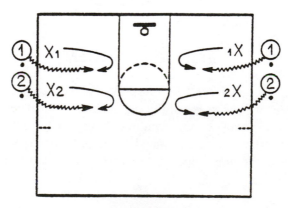

DIAGRAM 3-37

FOUR-ON-FOUR

Four-on-Four Drill: Diagram 3-38. Normal help-and-recover man drill is employed here and carries over to the zone. We don't want offensive penetration to go beyond the line of defense. We also don't want two defensive men to guard one offensive player. However, it's realized that they must help, but only temporarily. Hence, the term "help and recover" is usable in the zone defense. We use two guards and two forwards and their respective defensive men for this drill. The offense must try to penetrate and then pass the ball when they are close. For example, X2 must help and recover on the penetration of 01 and recover on 02. This is the player he's guarding when the dribbler pulls up the dribble or the split is controlled.

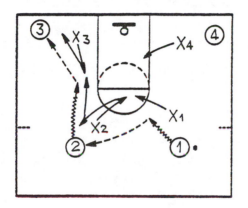

DIAGRAM 3-38

HELP-AND-RECOVER-SECOND DRILL

Help-and-Recover-Second Drill: Diagram 3-39. In containing the splitting dribble, the above drill forces two defensive players to stop the offense between the top of the circle and foul line. In the middle lane, there is the third defensive player waiting to react to the pass. The post offensive players are in position to receive the ball and immediately power up to the basket or dump off to the opposite post. They are allowed one step toward the ball. As shown in the diagram, X1 and X2 contain the dribbler, while X3 reacts to the pass. X1, the man away from the pass, retreats to protect the basket. This drill is excellent for lateral and retreating zone slides.

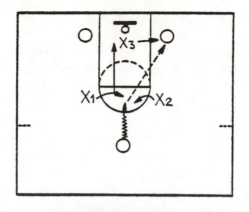

DIAGRAM 3-39

POSITIONING OF THE PLAYERS

Three-Two Zone

Positioning of the Players—Three-Two Zone: Diagram 3-40:
X1—The point:

a. He can be the smallest man on the team.
b. He should be the best ball-handler for the fast break.
c. He plays big men mainly to deflect high-post passes to the side.
d. He should have good, active hands and be very quick. This is probably
   the team quarterback.

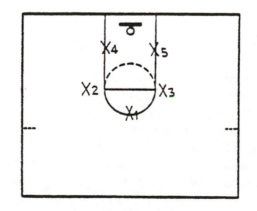

DIAGRAM 3-40

X2—The right wing:

a. A tall, agile player who must be able to move out quickly to start the fast break.

b. He must be a rugged rebounder and a tough player. He will be more involved than the other wing in the battle of the boards.

c. He is the key defensive player.

X3—The left wing:

a. A tall, agile player who is able to move quickly to start the break.

b. He must be the better ball-handler of the wings.

c. He must be the better defender, because most teams enter from the right side.

d. He must be able to hold his own on the boards.

X4—The right side:

a. He is the tallest player and possibly the strongest man on the team. He must be a hard-working player.

b. He must be able to defend the post area.

c. He must be a tough rebounder.

d. He must be able to cover the corner without curtailing his rebounding.

e. He is your "enforcer."

X5—The left side:

a. He must be the quicker of the two back men. He will be pulled more often to the corner than X4.

b. He must be able to rebound against the post man.

c. He's the best athlete of the two back men.

d. He has to be able to fill the lane on the break or be the first trailer.

Here is the basic alignment at the starting point:

The point—The top of the circle is the maximum extension, unless pressing tactics are employed.

The wing players—Their area is the "elbow," where the inside foot meets the foul line and foul line junction.

The back players—They straddle the lane above the box and can go as far away from the basket as the offense permits.

THE DIVISION OF COURT FOR COVERAGE

Division of Court for Coverage: Diagram 3-41. The defensive players are responsible for the ball in their area. There should be no confusion of assignments.

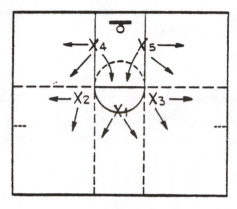

DIAGRAM 3-41

THREE-TWO UNIT ZONE SLIDES

Zone Slides: Diagram 3-42. X1 covers the man with the ball, OA. X2 and X3 hold at the elbow to prevent the ball from going through the zone. X4 straddles the lane, while X5 cheats up to be in position to cover OF. (This is called the ''up position.'')

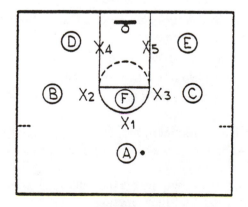

DIAGRAM 3-42

Zone Slides: Diagram 3-43. If the ball is passed from 0A to 0B, X1 slides to the "elbow" area to cover the high post. X2 covers 0B. He has one foot in the lane and must cover cross-court passes to 0C as well. X3 drops to the level of the ball. X4 slides to halfway between the corner and the foul lane, what we call a "cheat position." X5 goes under the basket.

Zone Slides: Diagram 3-44. If 0B passes the ball to 0D, X1 faces the ball, taking away the direct pass to the high post. X2 turns and faces the ball and remains in the passing lanes of 0B forcing a lob return pass. (We call this position the "blocking lane.") X3 drops to the weak side in rebounding position, X4 slides under control, taking 0D. X5 slides over in front of the post, facing the ball each time. (In some instances, we can play this player behind the offensive post.)

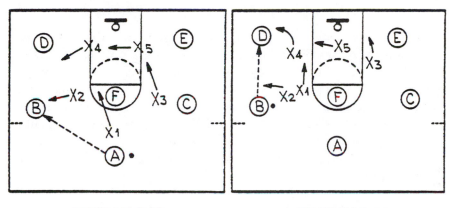

DIAGRAM 3-43   DIAGRAM 3-44

Zone Slides: Diagram 3-45. If 0D makes a return pass to 0B, X1 covers the high post, X2 plays 0B as the ball is caught, X3 slides at the level or just below the level of the ball, X4 returns to the halfway corner position, and X5 slides back in front of the basket.

Zone Slides: Diagram 3-46. If 0B passes the ball to 0A, X1 slides to the outside shoulder of 0A to prevent a quick dribble split, X2 slides straight to the "elbow" to prevent a gap in the defense, X3 moves up towards the "elbow," X4 slides over and cheats up to cover the high post. X5 will then slide above the box, straddling the lane.

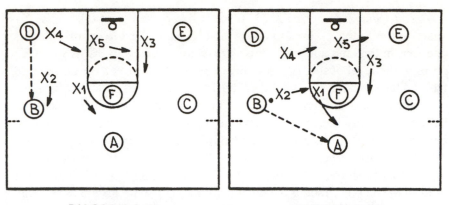

DIAGRAM 3-45   DIAGRAM 3-46

Zone Slides: Diagram 3-47. If the ball is passed from 0A to 0F in the high post area, X1 doubles up on the ball, X4 calls "up" and moves to play 0F one-on-one until the player passes the ball. X5 moves across to cover high and low and to be in position to move to the side of the pass. (The position and reaction of the two back men are the same as the tandem defense of the fast break.) X2 and X3 drop back to protect against a baseline pass. They will be in a 45-degree angle in relation to the high post. These two wings will cover the next pass to their side, whether it be out, front, or corner.

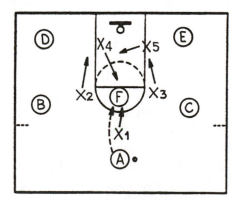

DIAGRAM 3-47

96

PLAYBACK

Playing zone has several distinct advantages over man-to-man defense:

1. It overcomes an opponent's physical superiority and athletic skills. Taller and faster players can be "neutralized" more easily with a zone.

2. Substitution is easier. Defensive skills needed for zone are more general as opposed to the specific ones required for man-to-man.

3. Zone neutralizes opponents by:

   a. Minimizing screening. (Defensive players follow the ball. Several can converge on it at once.)

   b. Forcing spot-up shooting.

   c. Minimizing the drive. (The middle and wings are generally clogged with two or more defensive players.)

   d. Forcing movement different from man-to-man movement.

   e. Slowing down teams with an active offense.

4. Zone enhances fast breaks

5. It creates a feeling of "oneness" for the team.

The Running Game

THE 76ERS FAST BREAK

by Billy Cunningham

Billy Cunningham was a high-school All American player from Brooklyn N.Y. who later went to star at the University of North Carolina (1962–65). An NBA All-Rookie Team member (1966), Cunningham was selected to the NBA All Star team four times in his brilliant career with the Philadelphia 76ers.

Cunningham became the head coach of his old team in 1977, making the playoffs each season. He was the youngest coach to reach 400 wins and won the NBA Championship in 1982. He retired at the end of the 1984–'85 season.

A coach has to be honest with himself. Just because he may like the fast break in principle, if he doesn't have the personnel to run it effectively, he's cheating both his players and himself. If you think you have the players who can make this fast-moving attack work, you will: 1) force the tempo of the game to a much higher level and 2) must be ready to run as much as possible.

From analyzing my teams over the years, I have found that the following characteristics define what goes into making a fast break team:

1. Good defensive players who are able to put a lot of pressure on the opposition. Defensive players bring on the scoring opportunities when they cause turnovers and block shots.
2. Good rebounders whom you can depend on to sweep the boards.
3. Instinctive runners. The players have to be able to react immediately, ready to quickly change from defense to offense. This quality is what most pro coaches look for when scouting a college player or looking for a player in a trade.

4. Unselfish players. It's the big men who generally get the rebounds, make the outlet passes, and block the shots, so we want them to be involved in the break too. Unselfish players are needed to give the ball back to these big men, when they fill the lanes and are in position to make the lay-up on the break.

5. Smart lead guards. These players have to know the abilities of their teammates and recognize when to get them the ball.

Remember: The most critical factor that goes into a fast break offense is a good, sound defense.

Before I start explaining what goes into our fast break, I'd like to say that I do several things a little differently than most coaches. Firstly, when we get the rebound, I want the ball passed upcourt as quickly as possible, not waiting for any guard to come back for the ball; this gets us right in the running tempo. I don't have any specific rules about which players are to fill which running lanes because I want the players to compete for the lanes.

Secondly, whenever an opposing player takes an 18- to 20-foot jump shot, I want that defensive man, whoever he might be, to first box out the shooter, see if he goes in for the offensive rebound, then release and go to the other end of the court. If there is a rebound from a missed or blocked shot, this player will be the one the team will be looking for to pass to.

I like to have my teams fast break after a steal, a rebound, or a turnover. In these cases, I employ what I call our "regular" fast break.

After a made field goal, I use the following fast breaks:

* regular sideline
* pull
* left
* right
* triangle

Players are numbered as follows:

01—point guard
02—off guard
03—small forward
04—power forward
05—center

REGULAR FAST BREAK

Regular Fast Break: Diagram 4-1. This break starts after a steal, rebound, or turnover. We want the rebounder, 05, to make an outlet pass to the point guard, 01, as near as possible to midcourt. 01 dribbles down the middle lane, while 02 fills the left lane, 03 the right lane, and 05, one of the trailers, goes down the three-seconds lane. 04 goes to the free-throw line extended. If the opposition should try to put pressure on the rebounder and delay the outlet pass, 05 has been instructed to take a few dribbles to free himself and then make the long pass.

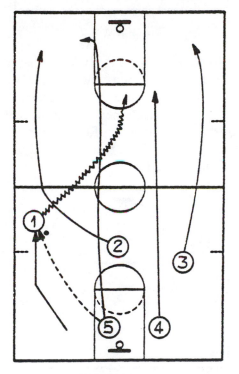

DIAGRAM 4-1

Regular Fast Break: Diagram 4-2. We don't expect to make a lay-up every time down the floor on a fast break, but at least we want a jump shot very close to the basket. If we can't get any high percentage shot off, the ball should be dropped down to 05. 01 dribbles the ball to the side of the court where 05 is standing. He tries to pass in to him while 02 goes on the opposite side. 03 fills in 01's spot.

103

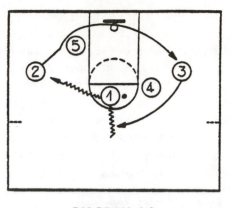

DIAGRAM 4-2

Regular Fast Break: Diagram 4-3. If 01 can get the ball to 05, he clears out, cutting in the three-seconds area. 03 replaces him, while 04 replaces 03 and 02 rotates. I have a rule on offense: After a pass or dribble, we don't stand still. Also, when we get the ball to the low post, we always create a triangle. This way, if the post is doubled up, he can swing the ball out to the guard or the small forward, so one of the those players can take the uncontested shot.

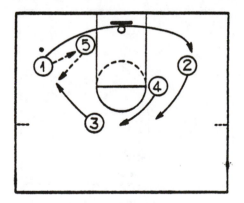

DIAGRAM 4-3

REGULAR SIDELINE FAST BREAK

After a made field goal, we run the regular sideline fast break, as well as options of a secondary break.

Regular Sideline Fast Break: Diagram 4-4. The center, 05, makes a long outlet pass to the point guard, 01, who then dribbles near the sideline. 02 goes on the same side as the point guard and crosses in the three-seconds lane, coming out the other side. 03 goes in the low post

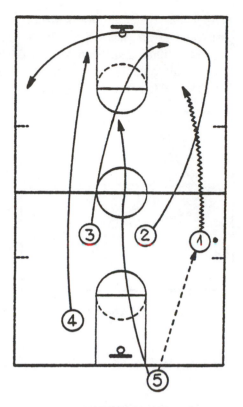

DIAGRAM 4-4

spot, 04 on the low post on the other side. 05 stays high near the free throw area.

Regular Sideline Fast Break: Diagram 4-5. If 01 can't pass the ball to 03, 05 screens down for 04, who comes in the high post area. 01 gives

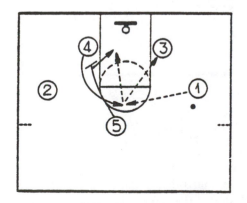

DIAGRAM 4-5

the ball to 04, who then has different options: he can shoot the ball himself or he can pass to 03 or 05, who then rolls inside.

Regular Sideline Fast Break: Diagram 4-6. If 04 hasn't any play possibilities, he passes the ball to 02 and then makes a screen down to 03. 02 can pass the ball to 05 or 03, coming out of the screen.

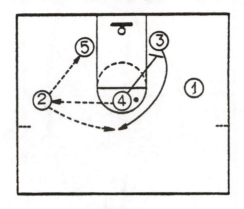

DIAGRAM 4-6

Regular Sideline Fast Break: Diagram 4-7. If nothing happens, the last option is a two-on-two play: 05 comes high and makes a blind pick for 02, and then rolls to the hoop.

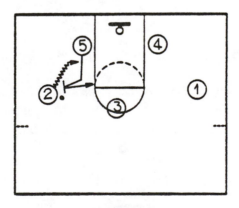

DIAGRAM 4-7

SIDELINE FAST BREAK: "PULL"

The point guard can also call different plays, depending on the situations. We have four other secondary breaks, pull, left, right, and triangle. All plays start in the same way as the regular sideline fast break.

In the "pull" play, we want to post up 05 and leave him playing one-on-one, spreading the other four players on the floor.

Sideline Fast Break "Pull": Diagram 4-8. While 01 is dribbling along the sideline, 03 makes a screen for 05, who then takes a strong position on the low post area. 02 and 04 then screen for each other or exchange positions on the floor.

Sideline Fast Break "Pull": Diagram 4-9. If 01 can't pass to 05, he changes sides to the ball: 01 can now pass to 03, 03 to 04, 04 to 02, while 05 crosses in the lane.

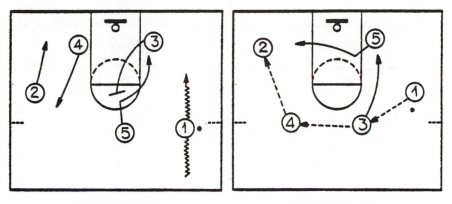

DIAGRAM 4-8   DIAGRAM 4-9

SIDELINE FAST BREAK "LEFT"

Initially 04 stays in the back court, as in the regular sideline break. He sets a screen for 01, or he can be the receiver of the outlet pass himself.

Sideline Fast Break "Left": Diagram 4-10. While 01 is dribbling on the left side, 02 cuts in the three-seconds area and runs his defensive man on the pick of 03 to free himself and be in position to get the ball from 01. Meanwhile, 05 posts himself low and 04 stays high.

Sideline Fast Break "Left": Diagram 4-11. If 02 can't shoot, we want him to swing the ball to 04. 02, using the picks of 03 and 05, frees himself, and by cutting in the scoring area, can get the ball from 04.

Sideline Fast Break "Left": Diagram 4-12. If 04 can pass to 02, he makes a screen for 03. He then goes in for the offensive rebound after 02 has shot. 02 also has his options. If he can't shoot, he can pass to 03 at the top of the three-seconds area or to 05.

Sideline Fast Break "Left": Diagram 4-13. If 04 can't pass to 02, he gives the ball to 03, and then screens for 02. At the same time, 05

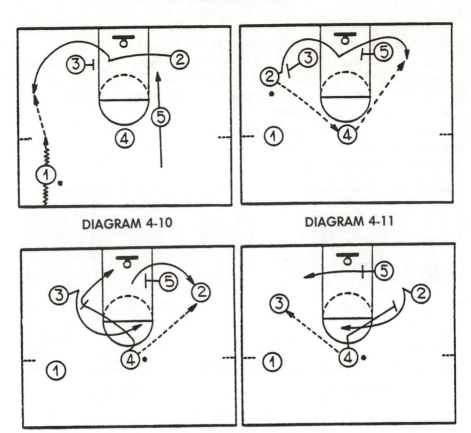

DIAGRAM 4-10   DIAGRAM 4-11

DIAGRAM 4-12   DIAGRAM 4-13

changes his position and goes toward the ball in the low post. 03 can now pass the ball to either 05 or 02.

SIDELINE FAST BREAK "RIGHT"

We use the same principles as the "left" play, but we tend to "curl" more on the right side.

Sideline Fast Break "Right": Diagram 4-14. 01 dribbles on the right side and tries to pass directly to 02 or 03, who cuts in the three-seconds area, and then "curls" around 02. If 01 can't make the direct pass, he gives the ball to 04.

Sideline Fast Break "Right": Diagram 4-15. 04 can pass the ball to 03 if he's open. Another option is to wait for 03 to come off the screen of

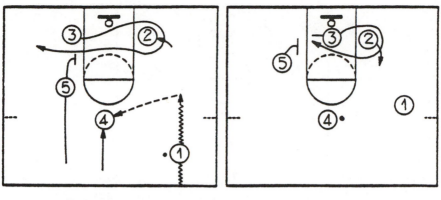

DIAGRAM 4-14   DIAGRAM 4-15

05. He can also pass to 02 or 05, who rolls into the scoring area after the screen.

SIDELINE FAST BREAK "TRIANGLE"

Sideline Fast Break "Triangle": Diagram 4-16. 01 passes the ball to 04 and then gets a blind pick from 03. 04 has the option to pass to 01 near the basket or to 03.

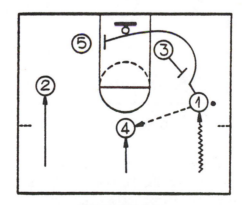

DIAGRAM 4-16

Sideline Fast Break "Triangle": Diagram 4-17. If 01 doesn't receive the ball, he sets a screen for 05, while at the same time 04 gives the ball to 03, who hits 05 coming off the screen.

109

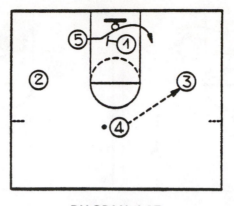

DIAGRAM 4-17

Sideline Fast Break "Triangle": Diagram 4-18. After passing the ball to 03, 04 screens down for 01 (what I call a screen for a screener). 03 can give the ball to 01 at the top of the circle, or to 05 in the low post position.

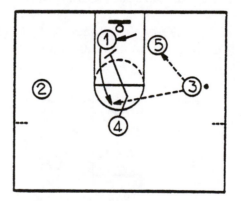

DIAGRAM 4-18

In practicing the fast break I tend to use the standard two-on-one and three-on-two drills. Also, at the beginning of practice, without using defense, I'll have the players run these drills full court.

As you can see, my fast break plays are relatively simple. The key to making them work effectively is to have unselfish players. You also need to have a sound, defense-minded team. If your squad defends well, blocks out, comes up with loose balls, and rebounds, you'll find many opportunities to get the fast break in motion.

PLAYBACK

1) You need the personnel to make the fast break consistently successful for your team. Because it works for another team, don't think that it can work for yours as well. If you do choose this offense, be ready to run as much as possible.

2) Ingredients for a fast break team: defensive-minded players, good rebounders, instinctive runners, unselfish players, smart lead guards.

THE LAKERS FAST BREAK

by Pat Riley

Pat Riley learned his basketball from "the master," Adolph Rupp, at the University of Kentucky. Pat was the team's MVP for three seasons (1964–67) and team captain his senior year.

After three seasons as a forward for San Diego, Pat Riley played the next six years with the Los Angeles Lakers (1970–75). He took over the head coaching job with the Lakers in 1981, guiding the squad to a 50-21 record and the NBA Championship that year. In 1984–'85 he once again guided the Lakers to an NBA Championship.

It seems very simple to speak about the fast break on paper. Actually, applying the X's and 0's on the court is much more difficult. Players have to be able to move instantaneously from defense to offense in a split second. And they have to know their roles and where they are expected to go on the break.

I think the fast break is much more difficult than either the pattern or motion offense. On the fast break the players are running at top speed, and while sprinting they're expected to pass, dribble, catch, and shoot the ball at these high speeds.

My philosophy is to "attack" at every possession of the ball. I'm a firm believer in running as soon as we gain possession. I want *every* ball possession to turn into a potential fast break opportunity whenever possible.

Breaking it down, I look to run on:

1. Shots missed by opponents

113

2. Shots made by opponents

3. Steals or interceptions

I don't like a freelance break because I want to have the team in a controlled situation every time; I have assigned numbers for each break situation.

Quickness, execution, and timing, as well as the *ability to read the defensive situation*, are of major importance for me and it's what guides me in the selection of my players.

I have found that you can have the quickest players on the court running the best fast break pattern, but if you don't have players who can consistently come up with rebounds and who are able to consistently apply strong defensive pressure on the offense, then the fast break will never become a mainstay in your offensive arsenal.

Our players are numbered as follows:

01: point guard, who quarterbacks the break

02: off guard, who fills the lateral lane

03: small forward, who fills the lane opposite the off guard

04: power forward, who works on rebounds and trails on the fast break

05: center, who has the same job as the power forward

The following is a summary of fast break situations:

a. Early breaks

b. Turnout into basic set

c. Dribble wing entry

d. Key pass motion

e. Dribble key motion

THE EARLY BREAK

Early Break: Diagram 4-19. After rebounding, I stress getting the ball out quickly to the point guard, 01, who must make himself available for the outlet pass. 02 and 03 fill the lateral lanes, and 04 and 05 read the situation. If we can go right in for the score, we will.

Early Break: Diagram 4-20. If the defense gets back, we'll use a play called "turnout." This will take us into secondary motion. 01 is in charge of the options: a) he can drive straight to the basket, b) he can pass

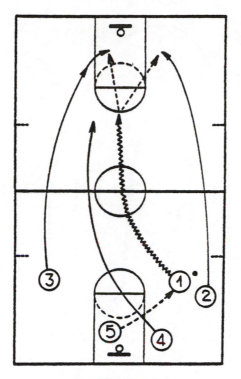

DIAGRAM 4-19

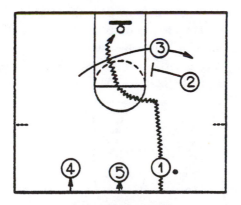

DIAGRAM 4-20

to 03, who comes off the pick of 02, or c) he can give the ball to 02, who rolls into the lane immediately after the pick.

Early Break: Diagram 4-21. If 05 isn't involved in getting the rebound and throwing the outlet pass, he can run the "turnout" or make a

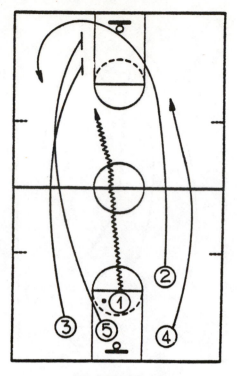

DIAGRAM 4-21

double pick with 03 to set 02 free. 01 can pass to 02 coming off the screen, or to 05, who clears to the weak side. 02, after receiving the ball, can also pass to 03 moving down the lane.

Early Break: Diagram 4-22. If it's impossible to take a shot, 01 can move to the wing, or pass to 02 or 04. At this point we're now in our basic

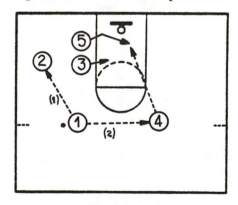

DIAGRAM 4-22

116

motion. The point guard will call the set offensive pattern as the defense dictates.

FAST BREAK AFTER A MADE
FREE THROW OR FIELD GOAL

Fast Break After a Basket: Diagram 4-23. After a successful field goal or free throw by the opponent, we want the center, 05, to take the ball out and pass to 01, or make a long pass to 02 or 03. If 01 receives the ball, we want him to dribble upcourt very quickly. 02 and 03 fill the lanes and 03 makes a "turnout" on the right side. 03 makes a screen for 02. 01 then passes to 02 coming off 03's screen, or to 03 who has now cut into the lane.

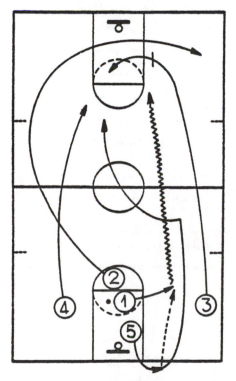

DIAGRAM 4-23

Fast Break After a Basket: Diagram 4-24. If 01 reads the defense and decides to change the side of the action, he makes a crossover dribble and runs the "turnout" on the other side of the court. 02 makes a screen for 03 and 01 can pass to 03 or 02, who cuts in the lane after the screen.

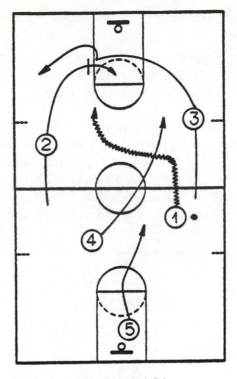

DIAGRAM 4-24

I have a rule for the two trailers, 04 and 05. 04 goes on the opposite side of 01, while 05 goes on the opposite side of the "turnout" movement.

Fast Break After a Basket: Diagram 4-25. 01 can pass the ball to 02, a wing pass. 02 then dribbles towards the corner and gives the ball to 03,

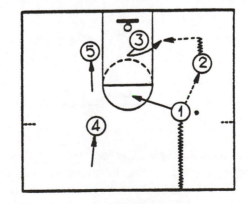

DIAGRAM 4-25

who has faked a cut in the lane and then rolled out to get the ball near the basket.

Fast Break After a Basket: Diagram 4-26. If 03 doesn't receive the ball, he cuts in the lane and comes out the other side. After passing the ball to 02, 01 screens for 04, who cuts into the three-seconds lane and gets the ball from 02. If this player can't give the ball to 04, he passes back to 01, who swings the ball to 03 on the other side. 03 then tries to get it in low to 05.

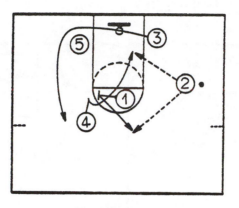

DIAGRAM 4-26

FAST-BREAK DRIBBLE WING ENTRY

Dribble Wing Entry: Diagram 4-27. Depending on the reaction of the defense, 01 has the option to dribble toward the wing, 02, who will post up very strong. 03 will cut in the lane and move to the opposite side.

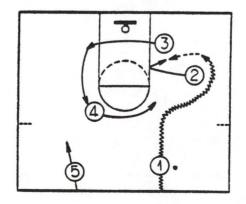

DIAGRAM 4-27

04 replaces 01 and 05 goes into a low post position on the other side of the court.

Dribble Wing Entry: Diagram 4-28. 04 makes a screen down for 02 and then takes a strong position in the low post area. 01 can now pass to either 02 or 04. Another available option: if 02 receives the ball, he can pass it to 04, who can cut into the three-seconds area, or to 05.

Dribble Wing Entry: Diagram 4-29. 02 can also pass to 03, and this player can give the ball to 04, who is crossing in the lane moving off the pick of 05. 04 can shoot or pass to 05. After hitting 03, 02 can make a screen for 01.

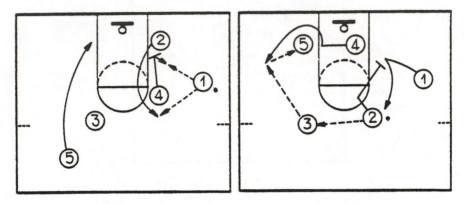

DIAGRAM 4-28   DIAGRAM 4-29

Dribble Wing Entry: Diagram 4-30. Other options (see Diagram 4-28) are: 02 can make a pick for 04 who rolls on in the lane, or make a blind pick for 05, who is trailing on the opposite side of the court.

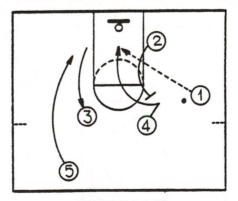

DIAGRAM 4-30

FAST-BREAK DRIBBLE KEY ENTRY

Dribble Key Entry: Diagram 4-31. If 01 can't pass to 02, 03, or 05, who steps into the lane after the turnout (see Diagram 4-23), he dribbles toward 04 (this is the key to the movement). 04 goes down, 03 clears out on the other side, using the screen of 04, while 02 replaces 01. 01 can now pass to 03 or 04.

Dribble Key Entry: Diagram 4-32. If 05 can't go down quick, he goes to the opposite lane of 04, moving in the low post position. 01 dribbles toward 04, who makes a pick for 03. 01 can pass to 03, 04, or 05. 02 replaces 01.

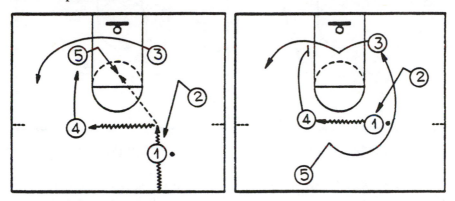

DIAGRAM 4-31   DIAGRAM 4-32

Dribble Key Entry: Diagram 4-33. With this team setup, 01 now has different options. He can pass to the wing or move into key pass motion.

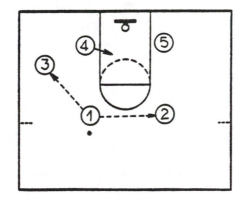

DIAGRAM 4-33

Dribble Key Motion: Diagram 4-34. 01, depending on the situation, can continue his dribble and go toward 03, who goes down and takes a strong low post position. 04 cuts in the lane, using the pick of 05, comes high, and replaces 02, who takes the spot of 01.

Dribble Key Entry: Diagram 4-35. While 01 has the ball 03 receives a screen from 02, and 01 can now hit 03, 02 (in the low post position), or 05, who makes a quick cut from the weak side.

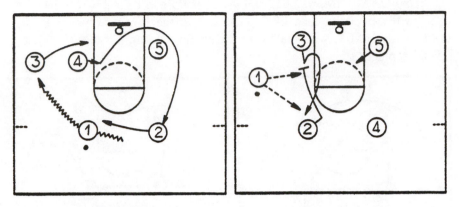

DIAGRAM 4-34   DIAGRAM 4-35

Dribble Key Entry: Diagram 4-36. From the set of Diagram 4-33, 01 has the option to reverse his dribble and make another dribble key movement, going toward 02, who will make a pick for 04. At the same time, 05 will step into the lane. 01 can pass to 04, 02, or 05. In this way, we have continuity throughout the offense.

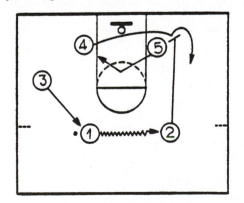

DIAGRAM 4-36

At every practice I work on the fast break, always stressing the fundamentals and proper execution. Three- and four-man drills full court are excellent ways of practicing the break, and are also great for conditioning.

PLAYBACK

* The fast break looks relatively easy on paper, but on court it's difficult to execute. Players are running at high speed and are expected to dribble, pass, catch, and shoot. That's the hard part.

* Quickness, execution, timing, and the ability to read defenses are qualities that I look for in my players.

* I want every ball possession turned into a potential fast break situation.

THE CELTICS RUNNING GAME: AN OVERVIEW

by Jimmy Rodgers

Jim Rodgers was a three-year starter for the University of Iowa. Following graduation in 1965, he began his coaching career as an assistant at the University of North Dakota under head coach Bill Fitch. In 1967 Rodgers took over as head coach, racking up a 39-33 record in the next three campaigns.

From 1971–78 Jim Rodgers was the assistant coach and head scout for the Cleveland Cavaliers, once again working with Bill Fitch who was head coach. Rodgers assumed assistant coach duties with the Boston Celtics in 1979, working for head coach (you guessed it) Bill Fitch. Rodgers currently is serving as an assistant coach to K.C. Jones and director of player personnel for the Celtics.

Through the years the pace of the game of basketball has continually increased as the athletes have become bigger, stronger, and quicker. Coaches and players alike have generally found the running game to be not only an effective offensive weapon, but also very exciting and appealing to the many fans of the game. Based on sound fundamentals, execution, and organization, the running game can prove to be extremely enjoyable to coach, play, and watch.

From a coaching standpoint, there is certainly more to achieving an effective running game than what meets the eye. Day-to-day preparation, persistence, and dedication to teaching the fast-break basketball style is extremely important. A firm belief in creation of a faster-paced game and a strong commitment to being very patient during the teaching and learning process is of the utmost importance.

One of the very critical objectives is to instill in our Celtic players what we term the *running habit*. Basically, this refers to the ability, determination, and discipline of our team, through a learned response, to effectively run the break at every opportunity utilizing all 92 feet of the basketball court. Our philosophy is simply a relentless pursuit to run the fast break successfully on all made or missed field-goal and free-throw attempts by our opponent. And, while playing at such an escalated pace, we stress and strive for intelligent shot selection as well as keeping turnovers to a minimum.

The *running habit* requires an excellent level of conditioning, both physical and mental, derived from a daily repetition of full-court fast break drills. Our drills may not be particularly unique to most coaches, but we have found that they fully prepare us to play the game at a sprint pace, yet confidently under control and with poise.

More importantly, our players believe that our practice drills create realistic game-like situations which not only thoroughly prepare them, but also can be carried over into the actual game experience.

The Celtic fast break philosophy requires the filling of five lanes, in most situations regardless of a player's position. We urge our players to communicate their lane to one another as it's filled, using "left," "right," "trailer," and "safety" as the verbal calls. This form of communication has helped us tremendously to quickly organize and designate the responsibilities of each player in relation to our "middle" push man. This player is most often in control of the ball as our break enters the front court.

Our *primary* objective is to gain an advantage fast break and ideally a quick, easy score. If this opportunity doesn't occur, the *secondary* action of our break is executed in order to maintain constant offensive pressure on our opponent's defense. Hopefully, we can create another scoring opportunity. By keeping the break alive with an organized secondary attack, we very often find an easy basket due to our opponent's slow defensive match-up or a specific mismatch situation.

The following drills are those which we feel are most important and fundamental to the successful development of our fast break philosophy. We practice with these drills every day using the whole-part method of teaching. Each drill enables us to teach particular key fundamental elements of the running game. Ultimately, as we build up the demands of each drill, the combination of the various elements leads to the full and complete execution of our entire fast break plan.

From *day one* in training camp and throughout the season, we use the following drills.

LONG PASS DRILL

The use of the long or baseball pass has proven to be a very effective and fundamental part of our primary break. This pass must be practiced often in order to be used with confidence and proficiency. It's important that we attack our opponent as quickly as possible. The use of this particular pass has enabled us to do so. The long pass has given us numerous quick retaliation-type points which can be very devastating and demoralizing to an opponent.

On many field goals, the emphases of this drill are to create and improve the following skills:

* Nearest (preferably big) man takes the ball out of the net
* He quickly steps out-of-bounds with head up and ball in passing position
* Clears away from under the backboard to allow full vision of the court and passing angles
* Makes eye contact if possible with a potential pass receiver who may release upcourt
* Executes an accurate medium to long lead pass to initiate the fast break.

On missed lay-ups or outside shots, the emphases are on strong rebounds; the rebounder must turn to the outside on the rebound side of the basket, away from traffic. Head up, he finds a receiver and executes a quick outlet using the medium to long range lead pass.

As shown in the following diagrams, the execution of the long pass drill is continuous action and also includes the practice of other fundamental areas such as dribbling, rebounding, and shooting.

Long Pass Drill: Diagram 4-37. The drill is initiated by 01 and 04, who make speed dribbles. 01 passes the ball to 0B, cuts hard to the basket for a return pass, and makes the lay-up. At the same time, 04 makes the same move with 0A.

Long Pass Drill: Diagram 4-38. 0B takes the ball out-of-bounds and throws a long outlet pass to 05. At the same time, 0A and 02 do the same thing. After the pass, 0B and 0A go to the outlet line and 01 and 02 replace 0B and 0A. The drill is repeated continuously.

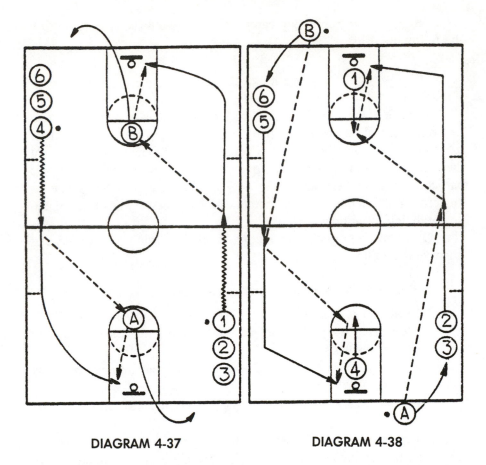

DIAGRAM 4-37   DIAGRAM 4-38

Long Pass Drill Jump Shot: Diagram 4-39. The continuity is the same as in the diagram seen before, except the player takes the jump shot from the top of the circle. The rebounders, 0A and 0B, make the outlet pass from out-of-bounds on made field goals and look for a long pass to 02 and 05. On missed shots, the rebounder makes a quick medium to long outlet pass. The drill can be varied by designating a spot for jump shots to be taken.

SIDE MIDDLE SIDE DRILL

This drill, although rather simplistic, is very effective in emphasizing our break organization as well as the filling and spacing of the lanes. As mentioned, we do stress that the players use verbal calls of "left,"

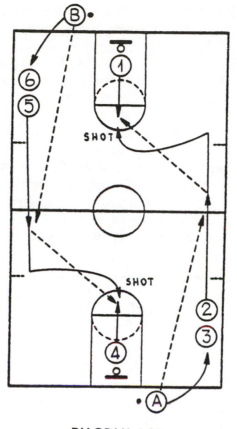

DIAGRAM 4-39

"middle," and "right" as they form a three-man rush. The "left" and "right" outside lanes should be kept wide, approximately one stride in from either sideline. The reason for such spacing disallows one or two defenders from effectively covering the three-man rush. In other words, *stay wide and force the defense to spread and commit itself.* Also, we have found that the best passing angles are achieved by maintaining a wide spacing technique. The two-handed pass and catch, rather than the use of an occasional long pass, is encouraged. The bounce pass is discouraged unless absolutely needed. We have found the pass-and-catch method leads to the least number of turnovers and greatest proficiency.

We prefer our "middle" man to pull up with the ball near the foul line area. This way we maintain the best possible passing angles to either of the players filling the outside lanes. They execute their cuts to the basket from the free throw line extended. If the "middle" man should penetrate inside the foul line, it means that he has totally beaten his man and is free to go to the basket.

One repetition of the *side middle side* drill requires the three-man unit to fast break the full length of the court and back. A turnover or missed lay-up means another repetition of the drill.

Creative and constructive variations of this drill are numerous. Build-ups of two, three, or four successive repetitions are excellent for conditioning purposes.

Side Middle Side Drill: Diagram 4-41. The players form three lines at the end of the court. 02 makes a couple of dribbles and then passes to 03, who gives the ball back. 02 dribbles until he reaches the three-seconds area, and then passes to 01 who goes in for the lay-up. The players who fill the left and right lanes both cut to the basket after they reach the free-throw line extended.

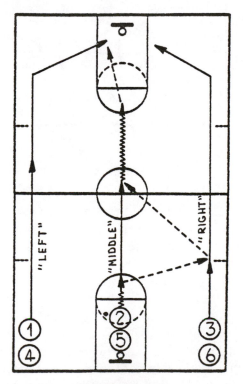

DIAGRAM 4-40

Side Middle Side Drill: Diagram 4-41. After the lay-up, 03 takes the ball, passes to 02, and goes on the right lane. 01 goes to the left. All three players repeat the movement seen before.

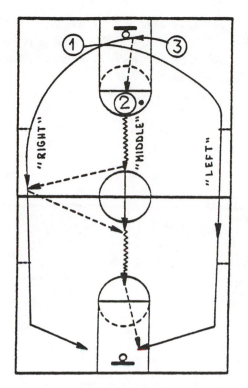

DIAGRAM 4-41

SIDE MIDDLE SIDE—TWO-ON-ONE RETURN

The three-man rush is now confronted with a two-man tandem defense. Verbal communication of lanes is again required and all fundamentals of the side middle side are repeated, with either a lay-up or a jump shot being attempted against the defense. Whoever takes the shot at the end of the rush break must quickly transition back on defense against the two former defenders who are now in a two-on-one fast break return. The other two offensive players who were involved in the initial three-man rush remain to become the next offensive tandem.

We vary this drill by not allowing the ball to be dribbled. The no-dribble approach requires that each player continually make mental pictures as to where his teammates are located. Each player must maintain body control and balance, as well as make accurate passes while on the run without the use of the dribble.

By disallowing the dribble in many of our break drills, we have greatly improved our passing and catching skills when moving at a rapid pace.

131

Side Middle Side/Two-on-One Return: Diagram 4-42. 01, 02, and 03 try to score a basket against 0A and 0B. The rule is that the man who shot the ball against 0A and 0B becomes the defender against 0A and 0B.

Side Middle Side/Two-on-One Return: Diagram 4-43. In the example diagrammed, 03 takes a shot and must immediately make the transition to defense against 0A and 0B who have become a two-man fast break after the rebound. 01 and 02 remain and replace 0A and 0B as defenders. 04, 05, and 06 form the next three-man rush after the two-on-one break is completed. 0A, 0B, and 03 return to the end of the line.

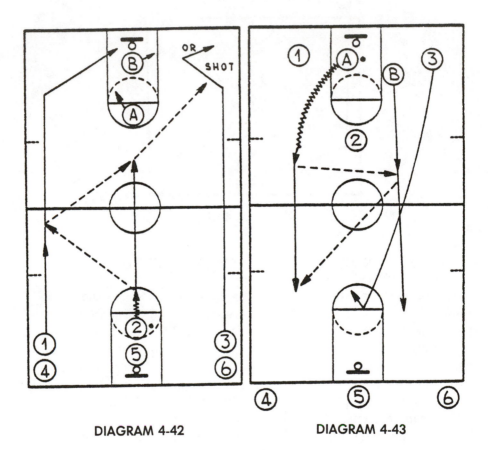

DIAGRAM 4-42   DIAGRAM 4-43

CONTINUOUS FAST BREAK DRILL— THREE-ON-TWO

This drill is one of our most important daily exercises. It requires that a continuous fast break action be maintained utilizing all of the previously outlined fundamental elements. Continuous three-on-two situations are an important aspect of the drill as is the quick transition from defense to fast break. The continuity of this drill is an excellent conditioner, and the repetition of each fast break fundamental situation can be clearly identified and critiqued from a coaching standpoint. The players are placed somewhat under the microscope for they must perform the various fundamentals of the running game.

Emphases of this drill are on break organization, decision making, passing, conditioning, and reinforcement of the *running habit*. We stress good shot selection, wise passing decisions, accurate ball movement, and a high percentage of successful fast break conversions.

The *no-dribble* variation to this drill has also been very effective and has produced excellent results.

Continuous Fast Break Drill—Three-on-Two: Diagram 4-44. 01, 02, and 03 fill the lanes and attempt to complete the three-man rush versus two defenders, 0A and 0B. 04, 05, and 06 form a line on one corner and 07, 08, and 09 form a line on the opposite corner. 0C and 0D are the defenders.

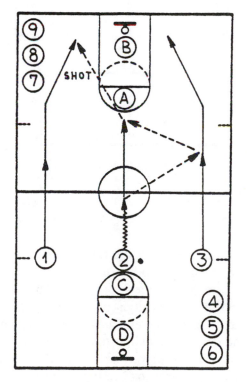

DIAGRAM 4-44

Continuous Fast Break Drill—Three-on-Two: Diagram 4-45. 0B rebounds and makes an outlet pass to 07. 0A, 0B, and 07 form a three-man rush against 0C and 0D. The drill continues as 0C, 0D, and 04 form the next three-man rush. After ending the drill, two players remain as the next defenders and one player goes to the end of the line in the corner.

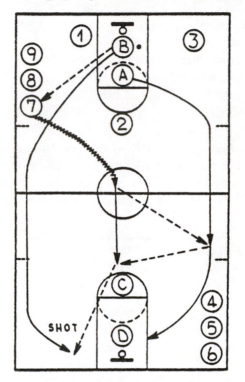

DIAGRAM 4-45

CONTINUOUS FAST BREAK DRILL—
FOUR-ON-THREE "FIND THE TRAILER"

By adding a third defender and a fourth offensive player (trailer) to the continuous drill, we move another step toward the development of our overall primary and secondary break structure. The fourth man (trailer) slice-cuts to a quick post-up position on the ball side as the fast break lanes are called and filled. We emphasize crisp ball movement in an attempt to find and deliver the ball to the positioning "trailer."

Mobile, strong post-up players are very effective when filling the "trailer" position and can thrive on beating their defensive man in transition for the quick post-up spot.

134

Continuous Fast Break Drill—Four-on-Three "Find the Trailer":
Diagram 4-46. 01, 02, and 03 fill the lanes and 04 slice-cuts into
"trailer" and post-up position. 0A, 0B, and 0C defend as the three
offensive men attempt to find and deliver the ball to 04 in post up.

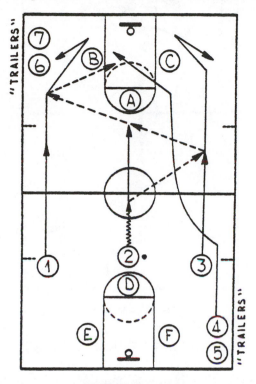

DIAGRAM 4-46

Continuous Fast Break Drill—Four-on-Three "Find the Trailer":
Diagram 4-47. The drill continues as 0A, 0B, and 0C, after the rebound,
form a three-man rush against 0D, 0E, and 0F. 06 slide-cuts into "trailer"
post. After each four-man unit completes the drill, three players remain as
the next defenders and one player goes to the trailer line.

The break drills which have been described and diagrammed are just
a few of our most used and most productive. Each drill, as stated before,
is designed to teach and refine specific fundamental *parts* of the *whole*,
which eventually, through repetition, develop into a total fast break plan.

Daily repetition of these drills and continued patience in refining
these fundamental techniques is extremely important and can't be empha-
sized enough. Players must become totally confident, conditioned, and
committed to successfully executing all elements of the break.

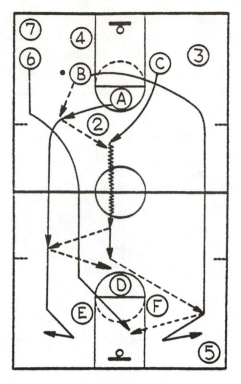

DIAGRAM 4-47

THE COMPLETE CELTIC FAST BREAK

Let's now look at the complete and final phase of the Celtic's fast break. First, in summary, our number one objective is to try for the quick score by use of the long pass, or by the quick outlet pass and the filling of lanes for the primary rush break. The "trailer" may give us the added possibility of an equally quick post-up scoring opportunity.

The fifth man entering into our *secondary* break is the "safety," and his presence can result in a well-organized, preplanned scoring situation at the very end of the break. Normally, the "safety" is that player who has inbounded the ball after a made field goal, or the player who has pulled a rebound and made the outlet pass to initiate the break.

The "safety" phase of our secondary fast break has unlimited variations and potential, dependent on how creative we desire to be from a coaching standpoint. The *basic* movement which we try to achieve is as follows.

Complete Celtic Fast Break: Diagram 4-48. 02 receives the ball from 05 and dribbles toward the offensive basket, but not in the middle of the court. 05 calls "right" or "left," and the ballhandler must go to the opposite side that has been called. 01 and 04 are respectively the left and right wings, 03 the trailer, and 05 the safety.

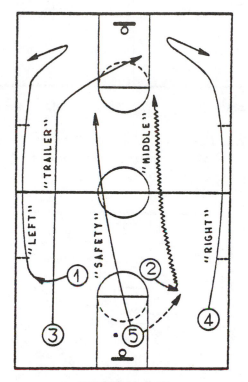

DIAGRAM 4-48

Complete Celtic Fast Break: Diagram 4-49. If nothing happens, 01 and 04 stay on the wing position and 03 cuts in the three-seconds area on the same side of 02, the man with the ball. He goes to the low post area. 05 receives the ball from 02, makes a cut in the lane, and gives it to 01. 05 then can make a screen for 02 (if 02 hasn't received the ball). 01 can pass the ball to 02 coming off the screen, or to 05 who rolls towards the basket.

Complete Celtic Fast Break: Diagram 4-50. If nobody can shoot, the ball is reversed, going from 01 to 04. 04 looks to get the ball to 03 in the low post area.

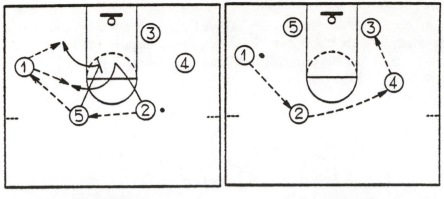

DIAGRAM 4-49   DIAGRAM 4-50

Complete Celtic Fast Break: Diagram 4-51. If 05 can't pass to 01, he gives the ball to 02 and then makes a pick for him. They play two-on-two, while 01 clears out to the other side.

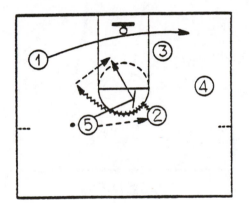

DIAGRAM 4-51

PLAYBACK

1) The running game, when it is based on sound fundamentals, execution, and organization, can be an effective offensive weapon. *Preparation, persistence,* and *patience* on the part of the coach in teaching the fast break will yield big rewards.

2) Players must have the "running habit," the ability to run the break effectively at every opportunity.

3) Daily practice drills creating game-like situations will best prepare your team for actual game experience.

4) The baseball pass is fundamental to the primary break. It must be practiced often.

Coaching Tips for
a Better Game

LAST-MINUTE SITUATIONS

by John MacLeod

John MacLeod was a three-sport letterman in high school and won a record 10 letters at Bellarmine College (Ky.). After two seasons of coaching high school basketball, MacLeod went to Oklahoma as freshman coach. In 1967 he was named head coach, guiding the Sooners to a 90-69 record and two NIT bids in six seasons.

MacLeod became the fifth head coach of the Phoenix Suns in 1973 and reached the playoffs eight of the last nine years.

As coaches, we are continually searching for ways to win and improve our team's performance. There are many times when a key basket could not only decide the outcome of a game, but also turn an entire season around. Quite often you will see a team have a great first half or perhaps even a good second half, but still come up short in the final analysis. It's imperative, therefore, to get the ball to your best shooters whenever possible. As we all know, some players shoot better under pressure than others. It's our job to see that the people who want the shots get the shots. Many times, especially when playing against man-to-man defenses, you'll have people who are open for a reason—the defense is giving that particular player a shot.

In high school and college basketball, with the many different defenses that are employed, it's often very difficult to get the ball exactly where you want it. This is when a disciplined attack becomes critical. It's important for everyone to understand their roles and be willing to execute for the sake of the team.

At the end of a game I believe that one of the most important things you must be able to do offensively is scramble. My reason is as follows. The opposition, having scouted you thoroughly, knows who your top guys are. Those players are going to be under great duress; therefore, when the exact pattern or shot doesn't go the way it's supposed to, it gives your guards the opportunity to penetrate. You must insist that they do so; they must have the green light to scramble if the play breaks. This applies not only to the guards but also to anyone who has the ball.

PASSING GAME LAST-MINUTE PLAY

For those of you who employ the passing game attack as your primary offense, you should realize that this style of play in its entirety isn't the panacea for offensive basketball. My feeling is that to set the passing game up properly, you need two or three crutches in your offensive attack. Otherwise, the nonshooter will always be open and the big guns will not be productive because they need help. In some cases, the passing game just doesn't provide the necessary help.

Below is a set of diagrams to give your passing game some relief at the latter stages of the game. In these diagrams you have plays that can easily fit your passing game attack. It actually accommodates three players: the guard who receives the downscreen pick; the forward who is involved in a split action; and the low post who has the option to go one-on-one in the low post. This play, as you will see, is initiated by a dribble and against pressure. It's a solid entry.

Passing Game Last-Minute Play: Diagram 5-1. 01 dribbles on the right side. This is a signal for 03 to go to the corner and cut around 05. At

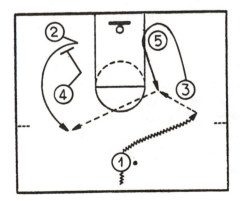

DIAGRAM 5-1

the same time, 04 makes a pick for 02. 01 passes to 03, who can hit 02 coming off the screen.

Passing Game Last-Minute Play: Diagram 5-2. If the defense switches—specifically, if the defensive man who was guarding 04 jumps to 02—03 then passes to 04 who's left wide open.

Passing Game Last-Minute Play: Diagram 5-3. If 01 can't pass to 03, he passes to 05, and then screens for 03. This player is then in position to receive the ball from 05 for the shot. If 05 can't pass the ball to 03, he can try to go to the basket by himself. On the other side of the court, 04 screens for 02 to keep the weakside defensive man occupied.

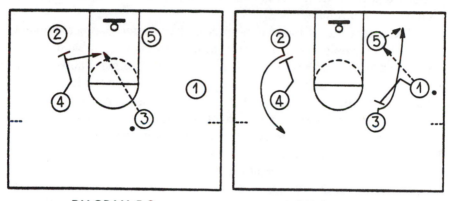

DIAGRAM 5-2   DIAGRAM 5-3

Passing Game Last-Minute Play: Diagram 5-4. If 01 can't pass to 03 because he's overplayed, 05 comes out of the low post area and makes a blind pick for 03, who cuts hard to the basket and receives a pass from 01.

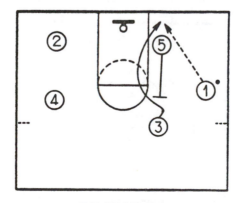

DIAGRAM 5-4

ZONE OFFENSE LAST-MINUTE PLAY

In attacking a zone defense late in the game, it's essential that your zone offense has as its base a disciplined passing attack, strong side to weak side, a high post either stationary or a player moving to the high post, and a low post.

Regardless of whether your offense is a stationary one keyed on passing, or your offense is a movement offense, the vital key is your ability to get the ball to the people who can fill up the basket. This may require five or even 10 passes, but it can be done. When it's executed properly and the correct shot is taken and made, it's truly a reflection of teamwork and discipline.

The recent use of the match-up zone has caused another problem when you are attempting to create last-minute shots. The problem here is that this particular defense gives the look of a man-to-man; however, in reality, you are attacking a zone. Recognition of this zone is difficult, particularly if you have young guards. This defense can make your offense look inept at times. It's important that you stay active offensively and don't allow your team to pass around the perimeter. If this happens, the only action you'll get offensively is an outside shot.

The match-up defense creates confusion, and you must realize that like all zones it has its weaknesses. *The match-up has a release point.* In other words, if your guard passes to the forward and goes through, the defensive man guarding him may take two steps with him and recover to his defensive position. When attacking a match-up zone, use diagonal cuts. And don't be afraid to use your man-to-man attack.

Zone Offense Last-Minute Play: Diagram 5-5. 01 passes to 03. On this pass, 05 cuts to the opposite low post area, while 04 comes to the opposite high post area on the ball side. After passing, 01 goes in the

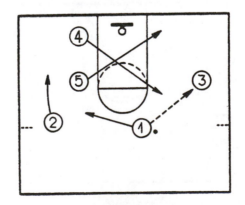

DIAGRAM 5-5

opposite direction. These offensive movements hurt the defense because they create indecision as to who covers whom.

OUT-OF-BOUNDS PLAYS

As you progress through your season, it's important that you have plays for certain situations and, if possible, plays that could cover you for every situation that may arise. For example, are you covered on the baseline? At ¾ court? Half court?

The following diagrams show certain shots that I hope will be of some value. These apply *only* to the man-to-man defense.

BASELINE OUT-OF-BOUNDS

Baseline Out-of-Bounds After a Basket: Diagram 5-6. We place two players, 01 and 04, at the free-throw line extension, 02 near the free-

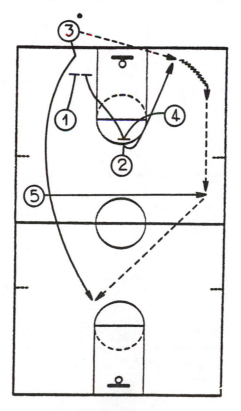

DIAGRAM 5-6

throw circle, and 05 at the 10-second line. When 03 slaps the ball, 04 makes a pick for 02, who goes high to receive the ball from 03. After screening for 02, 04 makes a double pick with 01 for 03. 05 breaks to the other side of the court, receives the ball from 02, and makes a pass to 03 for the lay-up.

SIDELINE OUT-OF-BOUNDS

Sideline Out-of-Bounds: Diagram 5-7. Against ¾ full court pressure, in a situation where we want first of all to make a safe inbound pass, we involve four players. The center, 05, is sent down on the offensive basket. 03 makes a back pick for 02 so this player can receive the ball from 04. 01 then makes what is called "pick the picker" or "screen the screener"; he screens for 03 who has previously made a screen. In this way, we have two possible receivers— 02 and 03. Eventually 01, who has rolled after making a screen, rolls toward the ball.

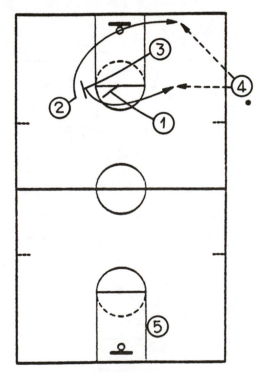

DIAGRAM 5-7

SIDELINE OUT-OF-BOUNDS
AT OFFENSIVE HALF COURT

Sideline Out-of-Bounds on Offensive Half Court: Diagram 5-8. 02 makes a pick for 04, who goes to the opposite corner and receives a pass from 03. 02 then picks for 05, who can get the ball from 04, or if this player doesn't have the ball, directly from 03. After the second pick, 02 turns and steps toward the ball and can receive a pass himself.

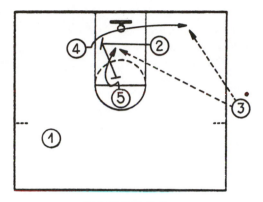

DIAGRAM 5-8

PLAYBACK

1) The ability to scramble, to break from a set play in the final minutes of a game and score is a key element in successful teams. All team members should be given the green light to scramble.

2) The use of match-up zones, a defense that appears to be man-to-man, makes it difficult for a team to create last-minute shots. Recognition of this zone is imperative in order to execute last-minute plays success-fully.

SCOUTING TO WIN

by Jack McMahon

Jack McMahon is Director of Player Personnel for the Philadelphia 76ers and Assistant Coach since late 1972–73. He is rated an outstanding evaluator of court talent due to his 31 years of experience in pro basketball both as player, coach, and general manager. He is a former coach of the Cincinnati Royals and San Diego Rockets in the NBA. He guided Cincinnati for four seasons and posted two second-place finishes as well as a playoff berth each campaign. At San Diego, he also served as the Club's general manager and had the most successful expansion draft in league history in 1967. In 1984, he was honored by his fellow coaches with a Special Achievement Award recognizing his contributions to the pro game.

Scouting your opponents is an indispensable game element that should never be ignored. Scouting will provide your team with technical information about offensive and defensive strengths and aid in your overall game preparation.

On the pro level, we try to scout our opponents twice before we actually play them. This way we can be sure of a team's offensive and defensive abilities. When scouting, we have our men pay most attention to the offense, the early break especially. This is because in the NBA with its 24-second clock, the tendency is to play a running game. Our scouts will see how the initial fast break sets up, then examine the secondary break, and finally appraise which solutions the team will use in order to get the quick basket.

Some teams, depending on personnel, will always look to get the ball in low to their center. Others go to a shooting guard, or their power forward. It's the job of the scout to note all of this and be able to suggest appropriate defensive strategies.

When watching a team's regular offensive pattern, a scout should be sure to note:

1. Which side of the court the team prefers to pass the ball to start the play. With this knowledge you should constantly harass your opponents on that side, causing them to push the ball to the other side when you play them.
2. Which player has the first option in the offensive pattern. Once you know this, you can try to keep the ball from him.
3. Which is the second option in their offensive pattern.
4. Which player gets the ball the most.
5. Where this player sets up most frequently on the court.

Scouts also pay a lot of attention to the signals that coaches use for calling the plays. The most often used words are "out," "up," "fist," and "down" followed by some number. "Motion" is also used and it designates the passing game.

Each coach also has his pet bread-and-butter play that he'll use for the quick basket either after a time-out or at the end of the quarter or half. You'll only have a few chances to chart this play, so be ready for it when it appears.

Basically, the scout should try to take notes on the principal four or five offensive sets. We could go for more, but it would be too much to expect our players to digest all of this information.

On defense a scout should watch for the zone and all of its applications. When and how does the team use it? Do they trap with two guards? Or do they rely on a guard and a forward combination? Noting these facts can better help you prepare your own strategy.

Over the past 30 years that I've spent in basketball as both a head coach and scout, I've seen tens of thousands of players come and go. From all of this professional spectating, I've arrived at certain criteria that I use for judging what I consider to be the "ideal" player. The "perfect" player has yet to come along, but many have reached my "ideal" stature. First of all, whether a center, forward, or guard, the ideal player has to be quick. This athletic ability is often overlooked by coaches. Yet it's the quickness of a player that will win many games for you.

My ideal player is one who can drive hard to the basket, at will almost, and be able to score in heavy traffic. There are too many players playing the game today whose basic (and only) shot is a jumper. I always tell young players that good things will happen if they can learn to go to the basket. Driving will:

1. Force defensive switches
2. Open the offensive game up for other players
3. Draw fouls

Standing outside and firing away at the basket is good, but being able to go to the hoop is better.

Another skill I look for is the ability to get the ball from Point A to Point B on the floor. When I was the coach of the Cincinnati Royals and Oscar Robertson was part of my team, the one aspect of his game that made him one of the all-time greats, was his ability to go wherever he wanted without fear that he would lose the ball to the defense. If you have a player who can move the ball like that, count yourself as very lucky.

An important aspect to consider when scouting guards and forwards is to note their ability to get off a good shot after the defensive player has forced them to pick up their dribble. This is a rare skill, especially when the defensive player is much taller. Another "must" that a player needs is the ability to fake the defensive player, cause him to leave his feet, and then get off a good shot.

Instinctive running, the ability to change from defense to offense instantaneously is another quality a player needs. When the ball gets in the hands of a player who has this knack, it's a beauty to behold. Julius Erving is a prime example.

Although it's not that difficult to judge offensive capabilities, it's usually very difficult for even a scout to estimate a player's defensive skills. Most college coaches (and high school coaches, too) try to hide a team's overall defensive deficiency by using a zone defense. Whenever I have to scout a particular college player as a pro prospect, it's really only a gut feeling that I can get as to his overall defensive ability.

When I scout college players for the pro ranks, I often run into many centers who are only 6'8" and forwards who barely break the tape at 6'5". Now, in this day and age, these heights certainly aren't pro heights. So in order to judge them accordingly as possible pro material I have to:

1. See if the college center can work outside of the lane.
2. See if he can dribble to the basket.
3. See if the 6'5" forward has enough talent to play the big guard position.

153

There are other signs I look for in a player that don't exactly relate to offensive or defensive skills. But they do tell me a lot about the player. This may sound strange, but I want to see if a player really appears to be enjoying himself when he's playing the game. Does he exhibit a positive attitude on the court? I've never seen a player go on to greatness or even become a good player for that matter who didn't first of all have a great love for the game that he was playing.

I also take special note of how the player reacts when he's on the bench. Does he cheer for his teammates? Or does he sit at the end of the bench and sulk? In addition to having the physical and technical skills, you as coach and scout want to have a player who above all possesses a good attitude. He's the one who'll dig down and give that something extra when it really counts. If you're lucky enough to surround yourself with players of this caliber, they'll not only make their contributions on the court, but they'll help in other ways, especially in keeping other members of the team from slipping into bad habits.

PLAYBACK

1) Coaches have their own bread-and-butter plays they use in specific situations. Get to know them and how you will defend against them.

2) Take notes on an opposing team's four or five offensive sets. Your team won't be able to effectively digest any more information than this.

3) In scouting a player as a potential recruit, look for quickness. This is a special athletic talent most often overlooked.

4) Look for a player who can consistently take the ball from Point A to Point B without any trouble.

5) Look for "instinctive running," the ability to change instantly from defense to offense.

6) Look for a player who can go hard to the hoop. He'll set up many offensive opportunities for the team.

PLANNING GAME SUBSTITUTIONS

by John Bach and Bob Zuffelato

John Bach played for the Boston Celtics in 1948 following his graduation from Fordham University. In 1950, he became head coach at his alma mater, guiding the Rams to a 262-193 record in the next 18 seasons. From 1968-78 he was head coach at Penn State.

In 1972 Bach was assistant basketball coach for the U.S. team at the Olympic Games in Munich. In 1978 he took over assistant coaching duties with the Golden State Warriors and in 1983 became head coach.

Bob Zuffelato was the head coach at Marshall University for four years before becoming the Golden State Warriors' assistant coach in 1983. Prior to Marshall University, Zuffelato coached at Hofstra, Central Connecticut State, and Boston College. In 1975 his Boston College Eagles advanced to the NCAA East Regional Semi-Finals.

The high physical and mental challenges of today's basketball demands a planned substitution table for the team. Most professional coaches have a table which meets these demands and yet has the flexibility to be altered after regular analysis. It is VITAL to the coach that his starting players *produce* in the minutes allotted. It is not unusual to have no further production in any extra minutes given to a starter. He must thus *go all out* with his allotted time—get those points, snare those rebounds, make those blocked shots— or else!!! The reserves are likewise held responsible for their minutes and also whether they held the lead, lost it, or improved on it.

The first estimate of a substitution table may be along these guide-lines: regulars to play 75% of the time, reserves to play 25% of the game minutes. Thus, in a 48-minute game, our regulars (at the start of the exhibition season) were programmed for 32 minutes, the reserves for 16, or half the time of those regulars. It provided great incentive for both groups to play well as they are held accountable for results in those minutes. Competition within the team was evident as well as high interest and anticipation of their entry into every game.

Further, a clear idea of the reserves' entry time made their prepara-tion incisive and certainly anticipatory. Their role was real, planned, responsible, and regular. The interest level of the substitutes was high all season. This table provided for 10 men on this regular basis. The eleventh and twelfth men worked with the first team in all practice games and waited for their chance.

The *most startling* result of this table was the rapid development of the younger reserve players. They would make mistakes in the early season but by January were more poised, more able to even start in the case of injury or illness, and more competitive in all drills and practice games.

Players NEED TO KNOW not only the why of individual and team defenses and offenses but also *when* they will be put in the game. This table gives mental stability to the wondering player. He now knows his role, his approximate entry time, and the minutes allotted in which he and his teammates must produce.

REMOVED, once and for all, is the caprice or emotions of a coach who can easily forget a substitution in the heat of a tight game, or the frantic pleas of an assistant coach to consider the substitution discussed hours (or days) before. The assistant coach handles the substitution table, reminds you of the planned substitution, and then allows you to delay the entry in case of a hot streak, unusually fine performance by the unit, or your own decisions to go a little bit longer. It's not etched in stone by any means, but gathers flexibility in the fertile mind and your view of the game at that point. It prevents an oversight which could be detrimental to the outcome. Obviously the team or personal foul situation can throw the timetable off, but even then the assistant coach knows who to brief (who to report is your choice) to go into the game and avoids the hesitancy which can be fatal in decisionmaking.

A staff review the day after a game reveals the actual minutes played against the planned minutes (see Chart A), productivity of the minutes of all your players, and any need for alteration. Experience has shown that a

Golden State WARRIORS

OPPONENT_____

PLACE_____

DATE _____

SUBSTITUTION CHART

1st QUARTER

STARTERS	ON CLOCK :	ON CLOCK :	ON CLOCK :	ON CLOCK :

2nd QUARTER

STARTERS	ON CLOCK :	ON CLOCK :	ON CLOCK :	ON CLOCK :

3rd QUARTER

STARTERS	ON CLOCK :	ON CLOCK :	ON CLOCK :	ON CLOCK :

4th QUARTER

STARTERS	ON CLOCK :	ON CLOCK :	ON CLOCK :	ON CLOCK :

CHART A

good month of games is often needed to put people into proper slots, experience "comfort" with the resultant offensive and defensive production, and see the calm, professional demeanor of the players emerge.

157

Golden State WARRIORS

OPPONENT_____   DATE_____

PLACE_____

SUBSTITUTION RECORD

NAME	1st	2nd	TOTAL	3rd	4th	TOTAL	PROJ. MIN.	ACTUAL MIN.	
CONNER									
FLOYD									
CARROLL									
SHORT									
SMITH									
BRATZ									
MANNION									
TILLIS									
JOHNSON									
CROSS									
ENGLER									
COLLINS									

CHART A (Cont'd.)

Here are Bob Zuffelato's comments on the substitution table:

As the holder of the chart and the timekeeper and communicator to the head coach, I have observed the following items which could interest you in your own plan:

1. It gives you an organized, structured plan that eliminates guesswork in substitution.

2. It still allows the head coach as much flexibility as he wants in making his player moves—you don't hinder his decisionmaking.

3. It motivates players who are included in the substitution plan to work hard to stay there, and it motivates those that aren't included to apply

themselves even more. Their incentive is a chance to get some "PT" (playing time).

4. It provides the opportunity for analyzing the success of certain combinations of players in a particular game at a particular time. We usually note when the second unit is in the game together and how they influence the game flow (plus or minus points).

5. It provides the coaching staff an objective method of changing a player's playing time based on his performance.

6. The preparation of the chart before the game takes only a few minutes—it's not a time-consuming task.

SUBSTITUTION CHART

The following is a substitution chart made up for all four quarters for a game played against the Houston Rockets. As explained before, we decided in advance which substitutions to make and at which time in each quarter.

SUBSTITUTION RECORD CHART

The following chart (Chart B) shows how we actually made substitutions during the game against the Rockets:

First column: minutes played in first quarter.

Second column: minutes played in second quarter.

Third column: total minutes played in first half.

Fourth column: minutes played in third quarter.

Fifth column: minutes played in fourth quarter.

Sixth column: total minutes played in second half.

Seventh column: total minutes of play projected.

Eighth column: total minutes actually played.

PLAYBACK

1) Use of substitution charts greatly enhances your team productivity.

2) With a chart in use, reserves will be certain of their entry time, making their role real, planned, responsible, and regular.

3) Use of substitution charts will help speed up development of your younger players.

OPPONENT __HOUSTON__

Golden State WARRIORS

DATE __APRIL 3, 1984__

PLACE __OAKLAND__

SUBSTITUTION CHART

1st QUARTER

STARTERS	ON CLOCK 5:00	ON CLOCK 4:00	ON CLOCK 3:00	ON CLOCK 2:00
CONNER		BRATZ/CONNER		
FLOYD	COLLINS/FLOYD			
CARROLL			TILLIS/CARROLL	
SHORT				MANNION/SHORT
SMITH	CROSS/SMITH			

2nd QUARTER

STARTERS	ON CLOCK 9:00	ON CLOCK 8:00	ON CLOCK 5:00	ON CLOCK :
BRATZ		CONNER/BRATZ		
COLLINS	FLOYD/COLLINS			
TILLIS	CARROLL/TILLIS			
MANNION	SHORT/MANNION			
SMITH			CROSS/SMITH	

3rd QUARTER

STARTERS	ON CLOCK 5:00	ON CLOCK 4:00	ON CLOCK 3:00	ON CLOCK 2:00
CONNER	BRATZ/CONNER			
FLOYD		COLLINS/FLOYD		
CARROLL			TILLIS/CARROLL	
SHORT				MANNION/SHORT
SMITH		CROSS/SMITH		

4th QUARTER

STARTERS	ON CLOCK 9:00	ON CLOCK 8:00	ON CLOCK 7:00	ON CLOCK 5:00
BRATZ	CONNER/BRATZ			
COLLINS		FLOYD/COLLINS		
TILLIS	CARROLL/TILLIS			
SHORT			MANNION/SHORT	SHORT/MANNION
SMITH		CROSS/SMITH		SMITH/CROSS

CHART B

160

OPPONENT _Houston_

PLACE _Oakland_

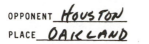

DATE _Apr. 3, 1984_

SUBSTITUTION RECORD

NAME	1st	2nd	TOTAL	3rd	4th	TOTAL	PROJ. MIN.	ACTUAL MIN.	
CONNER	8	8	(16)	7	9	(16)	32	23	
FLOYD	7	9	(16)	8	8	(16)	32	24	
CARROLL	9	9	(18)	9	9	(18)	36	39	
SHORT	10	9	(19)	10	12	(22)	41	43	
SMITH	7	7	(14)	8	8	(16)	30	33	
BRATZ	4	4	(8)	5	3	(8)	16	25	
MANNION	2	3	(5)	2	2	(4)	9	5	
TILLIS	3	3	(6)	3	3	(6)	12	9	
JOHNSON	I	N	J	U	R	E	D		
CROSS	5	5	(10)	4	4	(8)	18	15	
ENGLER	0	0	(0)	0	0	(0)	0	0	
COLLINS	5	3	(8)	4	4	(8)	16	24	

CHART B (Cont'd.)

CONDITIONING FOR
BASKETBALL PLAYERS

by John Kilbourne

John Kilbourne is a pioneer in athletic conditioning for motion sports and games. He currently is the only full-time conditioning coach in the NBA.

Kilbourne's education spans 11 years devoted to the study of Sport, Dance, and Kinesiology. Prior to his full-time appointment with the Philadelphia 76ers, he was on the faculty of the College of the Canyons in Valencia, California and Pepperdine University in Malibu, California. In addition to his work with the 76ers and UCLA, Kilbourne has worked with the 1980 U.S. Olympic basketball team, the Atlanta Hawks, Portland Trailblazers, Phoenix Suns, New Jersey Nets, Golden State Warriors, and the San Diego Clippers. During the 1982–83 season, the 76ers recorded one of their lowest "player games lost to injury" in the history of the franchise.

Most pro basketball players can't hit major league pitching, finish a marathon, or pole vault as high as a basket. But when evaluated in terms of physical grace, eye-hand coordination, strength, skill, endurance, durability, flexibility, agility, quickness, and reflexes, most experts say the basketball pro is the best athlete playing in sports today.

Included here will be some of the more beneficial exercises practiced by the Philadelphia 76er team. Selected are the exercises which should be practiced in order to increase performance and reduce serious basketball injury. *The exercises are a supplement to basketball practice.*

To achieve excellence in conditioning one must train both the mind and body. The mind/body relationship is the foundation of "complete" conditioning. Included here are exercises as well as research surrounding the conditioning topics. Reading and understanding the research will enhance and improve your practice of the exercises.

It is important to consider individual anatomical structures and capabilities while practicing the program. Don't force or push the structure of the body beyond individual exercise limits. If a player has a history of injury or anatomical disability, please practice the exercises with the permission of your sports medicine advisor.

FLEXIBILITY, RHYTHM, COORDINATION, RELAXATION, ISOLATION, MUSIC, BALANCE

Flexibility

Flexibility is the range of motion in a joint or a combination of joints. Lack of flexibility is one of the most frequent causes of improper or poor movement. It may also lead to many athletic injuries. (Swanbom, Don—1980: UCLA.) With poor flexibility, speed and efficiency are hindered. The muscles have to work harder to bring about maximum length. Extra work results in a greater loss of energy and will hinder the athletic performance. By increasing the flexibility of ankles, legs, hips, and trunk, greater speed can be achieved and energy conserved. The athlete will be able to run faster and jump higher. (Swanbom, Don—1980: UCLA.)

Flexibility training is the least researched and least understood component of physical conditioning. Says Donald L. Cooper, MD, "Strength, endurance, agility, and explosive power are the qualities most coaches want for their athletes. But flexibility, which often is overlooked in a well-conditioned athlete, can enhance all the other desirable attributes and help prevent injuries." (Cooper, Donald L., MD—1977:114.) John Jesse, RPT, decried what he found to be "An overemphasis on strength training at the expense of flexibility and specificity for the sport at hand." (Schultz, Paul—1979:109.)

In the early 1940s Thomas Cureton, PhD, proposed that "flexibility exercise may be given for conditioning in the sense that full range contraction and extension . . . is excellent massage and exercise for the muscles, producing both a physical elongation and a strengthening of the musculature." Such exercises, he added, "if built up to a sufficient dosage may condition the muscles, tendons, ligaments, and bones to a greater tensile strength and elasticity, a factor which is basic to preventing injuries in many sports.'' (Cureton, Thomas K.—1941:381.)

Almost 20 years later another pioneer in flexibility research, Dr. Herbert A. DeVries, found that ''Under certain conditions, the use of static stretching technique following unaccustomed exercise seems to provide some measure of prevention of ensuing muscular distress, and that static stretching seems to provide a useful technique for relief of chronic muscular distress such as shin splits in some athletes.'' (DeVries, Herbert A.—1961:479.)

The research of DeVries is very important and shouldn't be overlooked. When you invest time and energy in your conditioning program it's important to complete it with a thorough warm-down of 10-15 minutes. This will enable the body to recover and relieve soreness in muscle joints.

A good example of the warm-down principle is its application with thoroughbred racehorses. Seldom do professional trainers take their horses and put them back into the stalls after a workout. They spend considerable time warming them down to insure quality conditioning with minimum soreness and maximum output. The same philosophy should be applied to athletic conditioning.

A more contemporary pioneer in flexibility research is Jean Couch, author of *The Runner's World Yoga Book*. She says, ''By stretching the areas that have been contracted, you can reduce the amount of tension built up in the muscular system. If you don't stretch, tightness will increase and make muscles hard, nonresilient, and more susceptible to injury.'' (Couch, Jean—1979:84.)

Development

Flexibility is developed by ''stretching,'' slowly increasing the range of motion through which the joint is moved. The overload principle as applied to flexibility means attempting to progressively increase the range of motion through which one attempts to move. (Stigleman, Sue Ellen—1976:61.) When stretching, the athlete must also utilize the maintenance principle of conditioning to insure continued flexibility.

The development of an athlete's flexibility must be a part of every conditioning program. Donald Cooper, MD, insists, ''Stretching exercises need to be brought out from under the piles of weightlifting machine literature; properly taught; and put back into every athlete's year-round program.'' The wise coach will have his athletes use their flexibility program and stretch properly before practice. This should be done to avoid muscle strains and to maintain and increase the athlete's flexibility.

Flexibility Defined

There are three kinds of stretching: Static, ballistic, and reciprocal. Static, or slow, gradual, passive stretching is defined as the method involving a held position of greatest possible length. (DeVries, Herbert A.—1962:223.) Ballistic, or bobbing, bouncing, jerking stretching is defined as the method involving movements characterized by jerks and pulls upon the body segments to be stretched. (DeVries, Herbert A.—1962:223.) Reciprocal stretching is based on the ''psychological'' premise that contraction of a muscle is followed by lengthening relaxation, and/or inhibition of the antagonistic muscles.'' (Klafs, Carl E.—1977.) Despite strong opinions, a superiority of any one stretching method over the others has never been conclusively demonstrated. (Stigleman, Sue Ellen—1979:62.)

The conditioning program that follows uses static, ballistic, and reciprocal stretching techniques. A combination of the three is the most thorough way to condition athletes in flexibility training. With the use of ballistic stretching, the athlete will produce a mild sweat, provide circulatory warm-up, and be somewhat challenged and excited. Fred Kasch, PhD, Professor of Exercise Physiology at San Diego State University, agrees. ''I think we may have overdone static work at the expense of ballistic exercise. I favor a blend of both. Static stretching is boring. Ballistic exercise makes sense because so many athletic activities are ballistic in nature.'' (Schultz, Paul—1970:109.) Static stretching should always be used in early conditioning to limit the danger of exceeding the tissues' extensibility.

Another important characteristic of the ballistic program is the lubrication of the joint capsule. With the use of moderate ballistic exercises, the fluid which surrounds the joints of the body is sufficiently warmed up allowing freer flow of nerves and blood. The same principles can be applied to properly warmed up muscle. By warming up the body prior to an athletic event with moderate ballistic exercises, you loosen the musculature and allow for smooth and free passage for nerves and blood.

The entire prepractice conditioning program is coordinated rhythmically to music. The music provides an efficient timekeeping mechanism. The time in seconds of each exercise is very important.

Rhythm, Coordination, Relaxation, Isolation

"Because strength is easier to develop than other qualities, athletes have spent more time improving strength rather than developing speed, timing, balance, and other skills that would put their strength to greater use in performance. Who can bench press the most? Who can squat with the greatest weight? Who cares? What good is it on the football field or the track?'' (Jesse, John—1979:46.) John Jesse, RPT, a physical fitness consultant, believes that strength alone doesn't complete overall physical development. Athletes can enhance their performance by putting their strength to efficient use with the development of muscular rhythm, coordination, and balance.

William 'Little Bill'' Miller, a leading proponent of rhythm in movement, provides an excellent introduction to rhythm and coordination in his book, *How to Relax: Scientific Body Control*. "In the human body, the flow of the involuntary muscles is a beautiful balance of poise and rhythm. The beat of the heart, its contraction, its pause—its relaxing, its rhythm; the measured expansion and contraction of the chest in breathing is rhythmic. There is response to rhythmic sound, such as the tick of a clock, the steady drip of water. It's the muscles under our control which must be so relaxed and conditioned that they'll flow in harmony with the body's involuntary rhythm. It's impossible for us to produce rhythmic action deliberately. Only when a movement is repeated until it's performed with no conscious thought, no deliberate effort, is there natural rhythm. The rhythmic harmony of the muscular system—in other words, perfect body flow—permits freer circulation of the blood, which in turn tones up the body. And in the graceful movements resulting from the rhythmic balance, there is a saving of energy, and consequently less fatigue and greater endurance.'' (Miller, William H.—1945:24-25.)

For an athlete to develop rhythm or flow of movement, coordination exercises must be introduced into his conditioning vocabulary. Two conditioning concepts are necessary for this development. These are *differential relaxation* and *isolation*. Differential relaxation is a conditioning concept developed by Edmund Jacobson. It refers to relaxation of unnecessary muscle tension during movement. (Jacobson, Edmund—1934.) Differential relaxation involves decreasing unnecessary tension while maintaining the proper muscle action necessary for the movement being performed. This will allow for more harmonious movement flow with minimum energy loss.

167

Athletes often display excess muscle tension throughout their bodies. Relaxing unnecessary tension and concentrating on the areas that you wish to strengthen increases the efficiency of the body and allows for a more coherent flow of movement. Differential relaxation is an important element of conditioning. In addition, excess muscle tension requires a continuous supply of energy and can contribute to fatigue.

Isolation is an extension of differential relaxation. It refers to the ability to command movement in one area of the body while maintaining other areas. For example, basketball players can learn that they can move their torsos laterally from side to side while remaining stationary in the lower body. Isolation requires a high level of awareness of specific body parts and the agility to coordinate those parts against other body parts. The prepractice and postpractice exercises outlined here are designed to develop differential relaxation and isolation. Through the application of these conditioning techniques, basketball players can develop rhythmic harmony in their movement vocabulary. And with the rhythmic harmony there is a saving of energy, and consequently less fatigue and greater endurance.

There are many advantages to teaching differential relaxation and isolation to basketball players. For example, a player who has the ability to isolate his torso while maintaining a stationary lower body, can weave his way through opposition and increase his potential in both scoring and rebounding. A player who practices these techniques will exhibit less tension while playing and have an expanded movement vocabulary.

Rhythm and Music

Using music as an accompaniment while conditioning has many advantages. Jacques Dalcroze, the well-known Swiss music-dance movement therapist of the early 1900s said, "The rhythm in hearing or in creating harmonies is not separate from, but rather intimately linked to, rhythm in seeing and moving." (Kirstein, Lincoln—1935:286.) By using music with movement in conditioning, the basketball player like the dancer can enhance the expression produced by the central nervous system and amplify or narrow his results to their desired need. Martha Graham says, "Primarily its the nervous system that is the instrument of expression. This is the reason music, with its sound and rhythm, is universally the great moving force of the world. It affects animals as well as human beings." (Graham, Martha—1980:45-46.)

The use of music in athletic conditioning isn't new. There are recorded instances where coaches have improved their athletes through the use of music accompaniment. One such instance was prior to WW II when Boyd Comstock, the well-known track coach of the University of Southern California, was engaged by Mussolini to work with Italian athletes in preparation for the Olympic Games. Comstock worked tirelessly at the task, and it seemed almost hopeless until the clever American trainer hit on an idea. He had observed that the Italian athletes were fond of music. "Could the natural rhythm and coordination they showed in singing be applied to their conditioning in track? He had his athletes sing as they ran, jumped, and hurdled. Almost miraculous improvement resulted in their performances from this use of music in the athletes' conditioning." (Miller, William H.—1945:26-7.)

Another advantage of using music is the effect it has on the athletes' attitude toward practice and competition. Many pro athletes use music prior to their athletic event as a form of relaxation. This helps to free their minds and bodies of unnecessary tensions.

The prepractice conditioning program developed here is done to music. The rhythm of the music will keep the entire team together as they practice the exercises. It also enables the athlete to practice certain static stretching exercises for a prescribed length of time using the music as the timekeeping device.

The use of music in athletic training is still in its formative stages. The effect music can have on the harmonious flow of an athlete's movement and the effect it can have on the emotional outlook (relaxation) of an athlete, are worthwhile areas of exploration and suggest music's continued use in athletic conditioning.

Balance

Balance is yet another important concept in the training of skilled basketball players. Ida Rolfe, a leading proponent of balance in the human body, said, "Balance in the body doesn't reveal itself to the dilettante. It's a matter of intuition, experience, knowledge, and study." (Rolfe, Ida—1977: 12.)

"Balance reveals the flow of gravitational energy through the body." (Rolfe, Ida—1977:30.) Gravity is an enemy to a body without balance and symmetry, and is a friend to a well-balanced body. A balanced body is less subject to the forces of gravity. By aligning the body and developing symmetry of the structure, the body can operate more efficiently with less likelihood of injury and greater endurance. "A body whose components are symmetrically distributed around a vertical line dissipates less of its energy in meaningless tension." (Rolfe, Ida— 1977:204.)

The concepts of alignment, centering, and symmetry, all necessary for balance in the human body, are important components of the prepractice, postpractice, and strengthening exercise outlined here. Exercises that incorporate these concepts should be an integral part of a skilled basketball player's vocabulary. Their use in the training of players is seriously overlooked, however. Many injuries could be prevented and performances enhanced through the application of balance, alignment, symmetry, and centering to athletic conditioning.

In order to develop balance the athlete must take the time needed to develop correct posture. Posture (the position or carriage of the body in standing or sitting) is critical in the development of efficiency in athletics. The vertical line of the body must be maintained while the components of the body are symmetrically distributed around this axis.

Running and Endurance

Successful basketball in the 1980s will be a running game.

There are three areas of training that need to be developed in terms of running. They are: running skill, running flexibility, and running endurance. Running skill can best be developed by running. Herschel Walker, one of the greatest runners of all time, learned to run simply by running. He ran forwards, backwards, and from side to side. He ran up and down hills, slow, fast, and often. When he ran around the track, he often would pull a tire loaded with stones and attached to his waist with a long rope. This increased his leg strength and the strength of the deep intrinsic muscles of his pelvis.

It's important to make your running training applicable to the sport of basketball. This is called specificity training. Push yourself at all times. Always run back defensively. When given the opportunity, run the ball up the court and to the basket with speed, skill, and power.

Running skill can be enhanced by running backwards. Basketball is a game of movement in all directions, and running backwards will provide increased strength in the hamstring muscle and the deep intrinsic muscles of the pelvis. Maurice Cheeks, the 76ers guard, can run backward with almost the same efficiency that he runs forward. This is a tremendous asset to his fast break and to his superb defensive skills.

Flexibility is a key component to efficient running. The flexibility program designed here will enhance running speed, agility, and quickness. By increasing the flexibility of the ankles, legs, hips, and trunk, greater speed can be achieved and energy conserved, allowing an athlete to run faster and jump higher.

When developing running endurance it's important to remember that everyone has a certain limit to which his or her heart circulation system is able to provide oxygen to the working tissues (individuality). This limit is called maximum aerobic capacity. To develop endurance, one doesn't need to work at maximum aerobic capacity. A good measure of cardiovascular fitness can be achieved by working at an exercise intensity of 60 to 80 % of maximum aerobic capacity.

One suggested method of determining your individual exercise intensity is to calculate your maximum heart rate and then try to exercise at 60–80 % of this maximum. Maximum heart rate can be estimated by subtracting your age from 220. You can estimate your heart rate during exercise by counting your heart rate (pulse) for 10 seconds immediately following exercise and then multiplying by six to obtain the count for one minute. Workout levels of 60 to 80% of this are desirable.

If at the end of your practice you feel you need additional work on running, an exercise called "Seventeens" would be helpful. After practice and prior to the postpractice warm-down, the players run the width of the court 17 times. If you're concerned about their endurance intensity, check it using the aforementioned endurance guideline.

EXERCISE: HANDS, FOREARMS, AND SHOULDERS

Stand with feet in parallel position, the back straight, and the shoulders pulled down and back.

1. Shake hands briskly (16 counts).
2. Open and close hands while circling arms overhead and in front of the body. Each opening should reach complete extension and each closing should consist of a tight fist.
3. The opening and closing is done on the count of the music. The arms circle six times total (48 counts).

4. Repeat the entire sequence beginning with the shaking of the hands and circling of the arms. It is important that the arms remain straight as they circle. Total counts equal 128.

EXERCISE: UPPER EXTREMITY, HAMSTRING

Stand with feet in parallel position, the back straight, and the shoulders pulled down and back.

1. Reach right arm straight up, elevating the right shoulder (2 counts).
2. Reach left arm straight up, elevating left shoulder (2 counts). Repeat each side four times (16 counts total).
3. Reach both arms straight overhead and round over (8 counts).
4. Hang in this position (8 counts).
5. While gently holding onto the ankles, bend knees slowly (4 counts).

6. Straighten knees slowly (4 counts). Repeat the bending and straightening three times. As you straighten the knees, try to decrease the angle between the rib cage and thighs (quadriceps). Roll up in 8 counts to the starting position.

7. The entire sequence should be repeated three times. Each sequence consists of 64 counts. Total counts for the exercise equal 192.

EXERCISE: HAMSTRING, LOWER BACK

Sit on the floor with the legs parallel and the feet in parallel dorsiflexion (toes pulled back).

1. Sitting up straight, gently pull the torso towards the thighs trying to decrease the angle between the ribs and the thighs. Hold this position 48 counts.

2. It does not matter whether or not you can touch your head to the knees. What is important is that the back remains straight and that you gently pull the ribs closer to the thighs. Try to relax and breathe freely as you practice this exercise. Total counts equal 48.

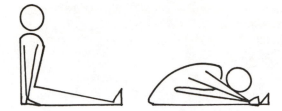

EXERCISE: ADDUCTOR (GROIN)

1. Sit on the floor, pull both feet in, and lift up on the heels of the ankles.

2. As you lift on the ankles, push your elbows into the inner thighs forcing the knees down.

3. Push the lower back towards the pelvis (anterior). The back should remain as straight as possible with the shoulders pulled down and back.

4. Once the above static position has been reached, hold 64 counts. It is important that the back remain straight and that pressure be applied to the inner thighs to increase the range of motion in the groin area. Total counts equal 64.

EXERCISE: QUADRICEPS

1. Lying on the left side of the body, extend a bent right leg as far behind (posterior) as possible. It is important that the leg stay bent and be pushed as far as possible behind the body. Holding onto the right leg with the right arm will assist you in pushing the leg behind the torso. The body must remain straight providing resistance to the stretching quadriceps. Hold this position 48 counts.

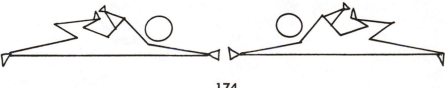

2. Repeat exercise with the left leg. Hold this position 48 counts. Total counts equal 96.

EXERCISE: ACETABULUM, SPINAL ROTATION, HAMSTRING, ANKLE

1. Lying flat on your back, pull the right knee in towards the right armpit and hold in this position for 16 counts.

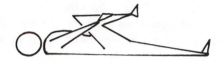

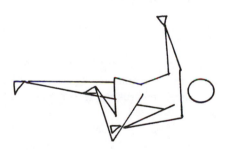

2. Holding onto the knee, rotate (circle) the leg which loosens and lubricates the joint capsule (acetabulum, synovial fluid).

3. With the knee bent, place the right foot on the side of the knee (keeping the left leg straight) and pull the knee to the floor with your left hand. Rotate the body to the opposite of the right knee and reach to the right with a straight arm, focusing on the right hand with your eyes. This will create a spiral rotation of the spine. Hold this position 48 counts.

4. Straighten the leg gradually, pulling it towards the chest. Leg straightens in 8 counts.

5. Flex (dorsiflexion, pull toes back) the ankle and point (plantaflexion, point toes down) the ankle 8 times each. Each movement is to be done on the count of the music. Total counts for dorsi and plantar flexion equal 16.

6. Rotate (circle) the ankle 8 times to the right and repeat 8 times to the left. Each rotation takes two counts to complete for a total of 32 counts.

7. Gradually move the leg to the side and return it to the starting position.

8. Repeat the entire sequence with the left leg. Each sequence consists of 144 counts for a total of 288 counts.

EXERCISE: ROTATIONAL SIT-UPS

1. Lie flat on your back with the knees bent, parallel, and in bent-knee sit-up position.

2. Rotate the torso from a stationary pelvis towards the right (keep the legs parallel) and continue the rotation as you sit up. The torso comes across the knees and rotates towards the left, then circles back to the ground.

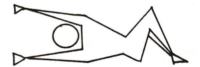
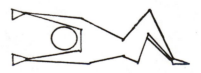

This is one rotational sit-up. This will strengthen the muscles which surround the abdominal area.

3. Try to do as many rotational sit-ups as possible. do the same number on the left side as you do towards the right. Example: 25 towards the right and 25 towards the left.

PLAYBACK

1) Prepractice and postpractice flexibility exercises will aid performance and reduce serious basketball injury. In addition to increasing flexibility, these exercises will also aid in rhythm, coordination, and balance.

2) Flexibility exercises should be a combination of static, ballistic, and reciprocal stretching.

3) Music plays an important part in the development of an athlete's rhythm. Try to incorporate it into your workouts.

4) Running skills can be enhanced through specific drills and increased flexibility.

BIBLIOGRAPHY

Couch, Jean.
"The Perfect Post-Run Stretching Routine." *Runners World;* April, 1979: 84.

Cooper, Donald L. MD, and Fair, Jeff.
"Stretching Exercises for Flexibility." *The Physician* and *Sportsmedicine;* March, 1977: 5, 114.

Cureton, Thomas K.
"Flexibility as an Aspect of Physical Fitness." *Research Quarterly;* 1941: 381–390.

DeVries, Herbert A.
"Evaluation of Static Stretching Procedures for Improvement of Flexibility." *Research Quarterly;* 1962: 479.

DeVries, Herbert A.
"Electromyographic Observation of the Effects of Static Stretching upon Muscular Distress." *Research Quarterly;* 1961: 479.

Graham, Martha.
"A Modern Dancer's Primer for Action." *In Dance as a Theatre Art;* 1974: section 5, Selma Jeanne Cohen, ed; New York, 133–43.

Graham, Martha.
"A Modern Dancer's Primer for Action." *The Dance Anthology;* 1980: 45–6.

Jacobson, Edmund.
You Must Relax; 1934: New York.

Jesse, John P.
"Misuse of Strength Development Programs." *The Physician* and *Sportsmedicine;* Oct., 1979: 46.

Kirstein, Lincoln.
"Dance: A Short History of Classical Theatrical Dancing." *A Dance Horizons Republication;* 1935: 286.

Klafs, Carl, and Arnheim, Daniel.
Modern Principles of Athletic Training; 1977: St. Louis.

Miller, William H., "Little Bill."
How to Relax, Scientific Body Control; 1945: Smith and Durrell, N.Y.

Rolf, Ida.
Rolfing: The Integration of Human Structures; 1977: Harper and Row, N.Y.

Schultz, Paul.
"Flexibility: Day of the Static Stretch." *The Physician* and *Sportsmedicine;* Nov., 1979: 109.

Stingleman, Sue Ellen.
"Conditioning for Dance." Masters Thesis, U.C.L.A.; 1979.

Swanbom, Don.
Strength: Off-Season Conditioning Manual; 1980: U.C.L.A.